THE CRISIS IN THE PUNJAB,

FROM

THE 10TH OF MAY

UNTIL THE

FALL OF DELHI

THE CRISIS IN THE PUNJAB,

FROM

THE 10TH OF MAY

UNTIL THE

FALL OF DELHI

FREDERIC COOPER

GYAN

Published by

GYAN

Gyan Publishing House
5, Ansari Road
Daryaganj, New Delhi-110002
Phone: 011-47034999, 9811692060
E-mail: books@gyanbooks.com

Distribution Network
gyanbooks.com
India, USA, Canada, UK, Australia

ISBN: 978-93-6433-171-5 (PB)

First Published, 1858

2nd Impression 2024

Printed at: Gyan Press, Delhi.

THE CRISIS IN THE PUNJAB,
FROM THE 10TH OF MAY UNTIL THE FALL OF DELHI
Author: FREDERIC COOPER

THE CRISIS IN THE PUNJAB.

P.

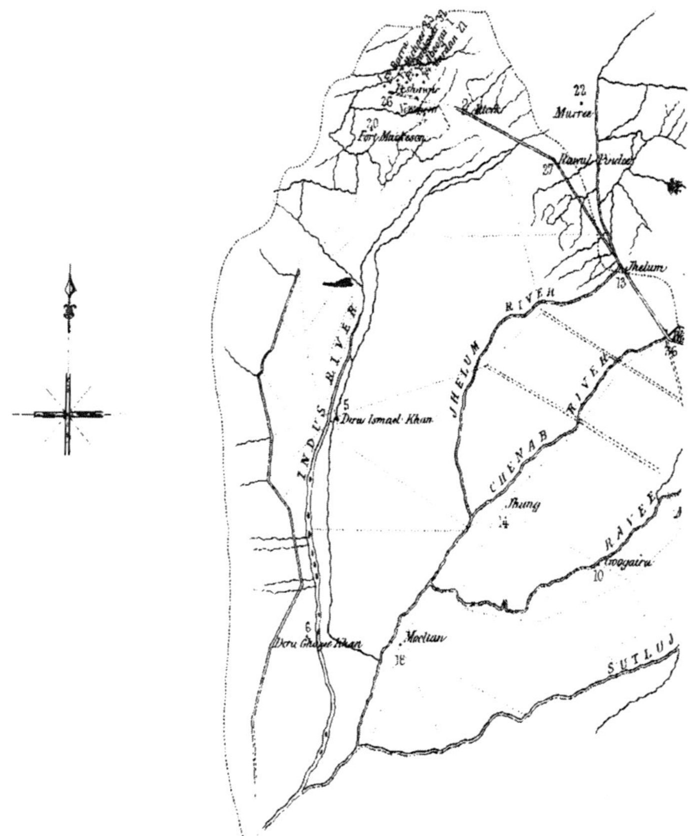

1. *Aboozai. Frontier Fort.* Station of 64th N.I. when disarmed.
2. *Attock.*
3. *Amballa.*
4. *Bul Ghaut.* Scene of Capture of 26th N.I.
5. *Dera Ismael Khan.*
6. *Dera Ghazee Khan.*
7. *Dugshai.*
8. *Ferozpore.* Scene of the Mutiny of the 45th & 57th N.I. & 10th L. Cav.
9. *Goodaspoor.*
10. *Googaira.* Scene of insurrection.
11. *Govindghur.* Fort close to Umritsir. Scene of disarming of the 59th N.I. & wing of the 9th L. Cav.
12. *Hurreekee.*
13. *Jhelum.* Scene of the Action between H.M. 24th & the 14th N.I.
14. *Jhung.*
15. *Jalundhur.* Scene of the outbreak & Mutiny of the 61st & 36th N.I. & 6th L. Cav.
16. *Kussowlie.* Scene of the Mutiny of the Goorkhas.
17. *Lahore.*
18. *Moolian.* Scene of the disarming of the 69th & 62nd N.I.

Published by E

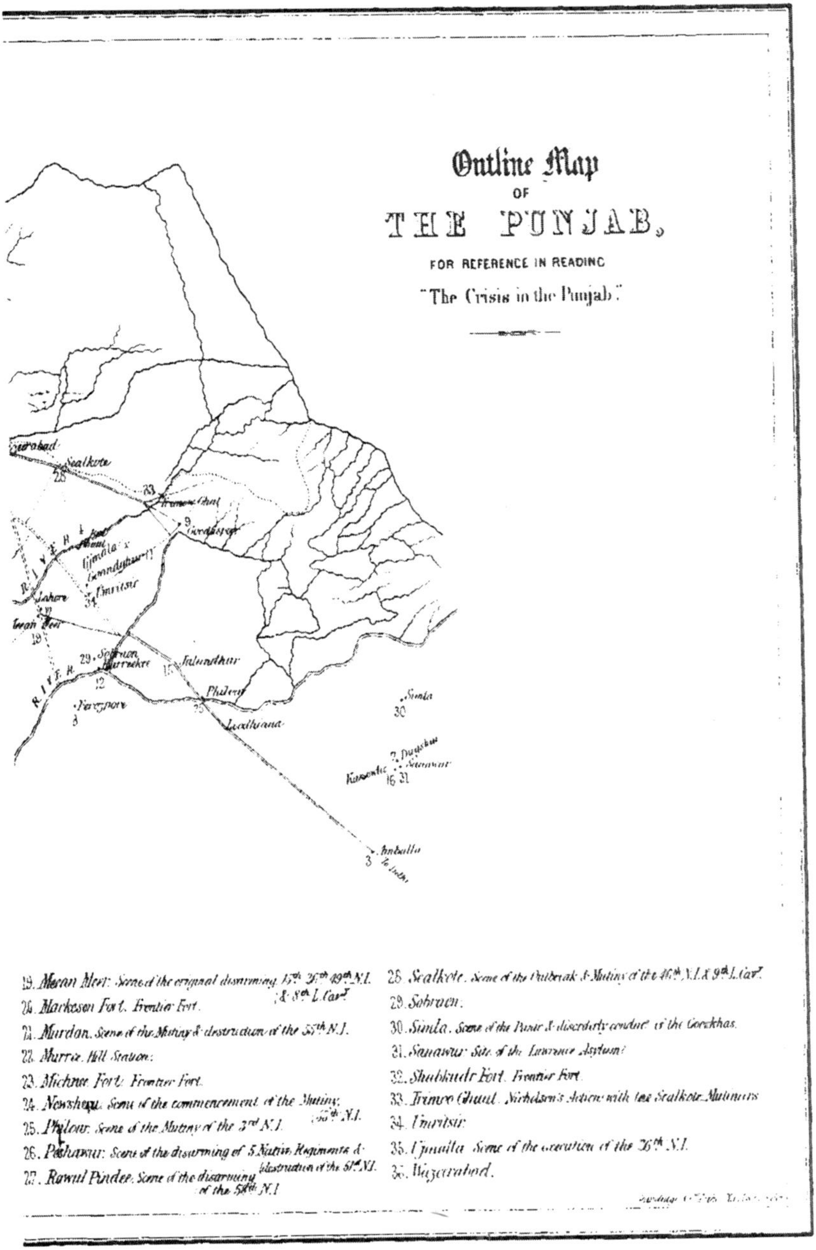

Elder & C° London 1858

THE

CRISIS IN THE PUNJAB,

FROM

THE 10TH OF MAY

UNTIL THE

FALL OF DELHI.

BY

FREDERIC COOPER, ESQ., C.S.,

DEPUTY COMMISSIONER OF UMRITSUR.

WITH A MAP.

LONDON:

SMITH, ELDER AND CO., 65, CORNHILL.

1858.

Dedication.

DEEPEST MOURNED AMONG THE VICTIMS OF THE LAMENTABLE AND GIGANTIC CRISIS SHINES THE NAME OF THE PATRIOT, THE SOLDIER, THE STATESMAN, THE CHRISTIAN, THE VICTIM OF HIS OWN MORAL CHIVALRY,

SIR HENRY MONTGOMERY LAWRENCE.

HIS LIFE WOULD HAVE BEEN CHEAPLY PURCHASED BY THE TEMPORARY LOSS OF A PROVINCE.

TO THE MEMORY OF HIM, OF WHOM THE WRITER KNEW NOTHING MORE THAN WAS PATENT TO THE WORLD—THE EXAMPLE HE SET,

THESE PAGES

ARE SIMPLY AND REVERENTLY DEDICATED.

DISPOSITION OF TROOPS PRIOR TO OUTBREAK.

PESHAWUR.—H. M.'s 79th and 87th.

Artillery.—2 Troops Horse Artillery, 2 Light Field Batteries, and 4 Reserve Companies, Europeans.

5th Light Cavalry, disarmed, 7th Irregular Cavalry, and 18th Irregulars.

21st Native Infantry, staunch; 24th N. I., disarmed; 27th N. I., disarmed; 51st N. I., disarmed, since mutinied and destroyed; 64th N. I., and Khilat-i-Ghilzie Regiment, staunch.

NOWSHERA. — Artillery Mountain Train Battery, Punjabees, staunch; H. M.'s 27th Foot; 55th Native Infantry, mutinied and destroyed; and 10th Irregular Cavalry disarmed and disbanded.

ATTOCK.—1 Company Reserve Artillery, natives, disarmed; 1 Company Sappers and Miners, do.; and Detachment 58th N. I.

SHUMSHABAD, near Attock.—17th Irregular Cavalry.

MURDAN, IN EUSOUFZYE.—Corps of Guides.

RAWUL PINDEE.—1 Troop Horse Artillery, natives, disarmed; H.M.'s 24th Foot; 58th N. I., disarmed; Kumaon Battalion, Goorkhas; and 16th Irregular Cavalry.

JHELUM.—1 Light Field Battery, natives, disarmed; 14th N. I. mutinied on attempt to disarm them, destroyed after a severe fight; and 39th N. I., ordered to Dhera Ismael Khan, and there disarmed.

SEALKOTE.—1 Troop Horse Artillery Europeans; 1 Light Field Battery do., H. M.'s 52nd Foot, 35th Light Infantry, natives, disarmed at Phillour; 46th N. I., mutinied and destroyed at Trimmoo Ghât; and 9th Light Cavalry, 1 wing mutinied and destroyed, and other wing disarmed.

JULLUNDUR.—1 Troop Horse Artillery, Europeans; H. M.'s 8th Foot; 6th Light Cavalry; 36th Native Infantry; and 61st Native Infantry. The three corps last mentioned mutinied and marched to Delhi.

PHILLOUR.—3rd N. I., mutinied and joined Jullundur mutineers.

HOSHIARPORE.—1 Troop Native Horse Artillery 4 guns with British force at Delhi, remainder of troop disarmed; 33rd N. I., disarmed at Phillour; 9th Irregular Cavalry, served with British force at Delhi; 1 troop deserted, regiment ordered back.

NOORPORE.—Half Company Native Foot Artillery, and Right Wing 4th N. I., laid down their arms at order of commanding officer, without the presence of the troops.

KANGRA.—Half Company Native Foot Artillery, and Left Wing 4th N. I., disarmed.

GOORDASPORE.—2nd Irregular Cavalry.

FEROZEPORE.—1 Company European Foot Artillery; 1 European Light Field Battery; H. M.'s 61st Foot; 10th Light Cavalry, disarmed, subsequently mutinied, portion escaped to Delhi; 45th N. I. and 57th N. I., the first mutinied, and disbanded.

MOOLTAN.—1 Troop Native Horse Artillery, disarmed; 62nd N. I., disarmed; 69th N. I., disarmed; and 1st Irregular Cavalry.

UMBALLAH.—2 Troops European Horse Artillery; H. M.'s 9th Light Dragoons; 4th Lancers, natives, portion disarmed, and portion employed on service; 5th N. I., disarmed; and 60th N. I., mutinied *en route* to Rohtuck; marched into Delhi.

JUTTOGH, NEAR SIMLA, HIMALAYAS.—Nusseree Battalion, temporary disaffection—order restored—regiment employed on service.

DUGSHAIE HIMALAYAS.—1st Brigade Bengal Fusiliers.

KUSSOWLIE HIMALAYAS.—H. M.'s 75th Foot.

SUBATHOO HIMALAYAS.—2nd European Bengal Fusiliers.

THE PUNJAB FRONTIER guarded by four local regiments of Sikh Infantry, besides the Guide Corps at Murdan. Punjab Irregular force consisted of 4 Light Field Batteries, 5 Regiments of Cavalry, and 6 Regiments of Infantry.

LAHORE.—2 Troops Horse Artillery, Europeans; 4 Companies Reserve Artillery, Europeans; H. M.'s 81st Foot; 8th Light Cavalry, disarmed; 16th N. I., disarmed; and 26th Light Infantry, disarmed—subsequently mutinied—and destroyed at Ball Ghat; and 49th, disarmed.

UMRITSUR.—1 Light Field Battery, natives, disarmed; 59th N. I., disarmed; 1 Company European Reserve Artillery in the fort of Govindgurh.

DISPOSITION OF TROOPS SUBSEQUENT TO OUTBREAK.

APPROXIMATED STATEMENT of Poorbeah Soldiery and reliable Troops to watch them in the Punjab.

Stations.	Details.	Arm'd	Dis-armed	Watched by	Eur.	Native
Peshawur & Attock	5th Cav.	3,000	4,000	2 troops Horse Artillery } 2 Batteries Artillery }	340	—
	24th N. I.					
	27th ,,			Peshawur Mountain Train	—	100
	21st ,,			Peshawur Light Horse .	160	—
	64th ,,			2 European Regts . .	1,480	—
	Khelat-i-Ghilzie			2 New Punjab Corps .	—	1,200
	7th and 15th Irr. Cav.			And at Attock and Noushera.		
				1 European Regt. . .	590	—
	500 Art.			1 New Punjab Corps .	—	600
Murdan .	2nd P. C.	150	—	2 Punjab Cavalry . .	—	150
				5 Punjab Infantry .	—	600
Kohat .	3 Cos. 58th N. I.	250	250	3 and 6 Punjab Infantry	—	1,000
				1 Battery Punjab Art. .	—	100
	Men of 3rd & 6th S.I.			1 New Punjab Corps .	—	600
Bunnoo .	9th I. C.	350	100	1 Punjab Battery . .	—	100
	3rd Sikhs			3 Sikh Infantry . .	—	700
Dera Ismail Khan	39th N. I.	250	800	1 Punjab Battery . .	—	100
	5th P. C.			1 Punjab Cavalry .	—	100
				1 New Punjab Corps .	—	600
Dera Ghazee Khan	4th P. C.	300	—	2 guns P. I Force . .	—	40
	1st Sikhs			1 Sikh Infantry . .	—	700
Mooltan .	62nd N. I.	500	1,700	1 troop Horse Art., new	100	—
	69th N. I.			1 Bombay Fus., wing .	350	—
	1st I. C.			1 new Punjab corps .	—	600
Rawul Pindee . .	58th N. I., 7 Cos.	200	550	1 Battery Artillery . .	100	—
				H. M.'s 24th Regt., part.	240	—
	17th I.C. pt.			1 New Punjab Corps .	—	600
Murree .	—	—	—	Convalescent Depot .	150	—
				Detach. 2nd Sikhs and of New Punjab Corps .	—	500
Hazarah .	—	—	—	Hazarah Mountain Train	—	80
				Detach. 2nd Sikhs and of New Punjab Corps .	—	500

Stations.	Details.	Arm'd	Dis-armed	Watched by	Eur.	Native
Meean Meer includes Lahore	16th N. I. 49th N. I. 8th L. C. 9th L. C., part	—	2,300	1 troop Horse Artillery } 1 Battery Artillery }	200	—
				H. M.'s 81st Regt., part	350	—
				1 New Punjab Corps .	—	600
				And at Annarkullic and Lahore Fort		
				Lahore Light Horse .	80	—
				European Inf. and Art. .	200	—
				New Punjab Corps .	—	600
Umritsur includes Fort Govind-gurh	59th N. I. 35th N. I. 5 Co. 8 Batt. Art.	—	1,700	Moveable Column . .	50	150
				Detail—Art. and Inf. .	150	—
Jullundur and Hooshiar-poor	33rd N. I. 16th I. C. 4th N. I., wing	400	1,200	Detach. 24th Regt. .	200	—
				3 guns Horse Art. . .	50	—
				1 New Punjab Corps .	—	600
Kangra .	4th N. I., wing	—	400	Convalescents . .	—	—
Goordaspore	2nd I. C.	400	—	—	—	—
Ferozepoor	10th L. C., part.	—	120	1 Bombay Fus., wing .	350	—
				Detail—Art., 6 guns .	100	—
				1 New Corps . . .	—	600
Umballah .	—	In Prison.		Detach. 8th Queen's Regt.	250	—
				1 New Punjab Corps .	—	600
Phillour and Loordianah	—	—	—	1 New Punjab Corps, and Detach. of Inf. and Art.	130	800
		5,800	13,120		5,620	13,320
		18,920			18,940	

PREFACE.

The following pages pretend to nothing more ambitious than a faithful description of the events which occurred in the Punjab during four of the most memorable months which have ever ran their course in India.

They were penned in spare half-hours of leisure snatched from time occupied in heavy official duties, and their only merit lies in the various facts which have been most obligingly placed at the disposal of the writer.

It is not presumed to enter into any discussion of the multitudinous causes of the mutiny of the Bengal army, or to expatiate on theories for its re-organization; much less is it attempted to criticise the conduct of individual regiments: the desire of the writer is to show how the emergencies, as they affected the Punjab, were grappled with.

The metamorphosis effected in the military arrangements of the Punjab, within four months, will perhaps carry conviction to the mind of the statistician; even if a perusal of the volume should fall short of depicting adequately the bold measures which completed so astounding a change, and the nature of the circumstances which rendered them imperative. In the first list prefixed to this chapter will be observed the enormous force of 30,000 men of Infantry, Cavalry, and Company's Foot Artillery, chiefly composed of the "Poorbeah" element, which, at the commencement of the outbreak, was in a ferment over the whole valley of the Ganges. He will observe in the next statement the altered arrangement.

On the morning of the 11th of May, the first intelligence of the revolt at Meerut and the massacre at Delhi was flashed to the seat of the Punjab Government at the ancient capital of Lahore. Notwithstanding the vague foreshadowings of disaster with which the events at Berhampore and at Barrackpore, the successive fires at various military stations, and other rapid and unmistakeable symptoms of wide-spread disaffection had clouded the public mind, there can be no doubt that the seizure of Delhi and its concomitant tragedies burst upon Anglo-Indian Society like a thunder clap.

Under the full force of the first shock of so stupendous a crisis, something akin to a panic was produced. The least reflecting required no Daniel to interpret the dread symbols. The hot weather had set in. Territorial expansion and aggrandizement had reached its extreme limits, while the force of European troops had dwindled to its extreme minimum. India was weaker by two cavalry and four infantry European regiments. Cholera had decimated European troops last year, and their vacancies had not been filled up. In Bombay, the European force was not nearly up to the ordinary peace establishment. The first layer of civilization had hardly been spread over Oude; in the capital of which was but one single European regiment. The Bombay army was half composed of Poorbeahs. The Persian treaty had scarcely been ratified, while the inflammatory proclamation of the Shah, calling on all the faithful to oust the *treacherous tribe of the British*, was fresh in the memory of every Mahomedan in India. Delicate negociations were still pending with Dost Mahomed at Kabul; and the lives of the gallant Lumsden and his party seemed hanging upon a straw. From Delhi to Calcutta lay a clear field for mutiny and insurrection. The sepoy army had become intoxicated with their sense of power. Every heart prayed, though few dared hope, for the Christians scattered over that boundless area. Every one anticipated the enormities that might occur. The silence which followed from the abrupt stoppage of electric telegraph communication, was even more oppressive than the after budgets of dismal tidings, and added to the gloomy forebodings. The vagueness, the immensity, the closeness of the peril, exaggerated alarm. Such were the feelings at Lahore.

The actual incidents of those days are generally familiar in the dread outline. Had all Hindoostan been lapped in repose, as in England was fondly hoped, these incidents in the land of the five rivers would have marked an era in a century. In the presence of Hindoostan convulsed, and anarchy raging, the calamities of the Punjab, though individually terrible, its trials though almost preterhuman, seem absolutely dwarfed. Looking around brought scanty solace.

The people of the Punjab are composed of what were once the most chivalrous, the fiercest, and the most inveterate of our enemies. What impression even, supposing no previous concert, would passing events create in their minds? The old Sikh nobility were rapidly, though gently, sinking into decay; and though cadets of families, once pillars of Runjeet's throne, survived (hereditary mementos of times almost traditionary, so swift had been the obliteration) there were still some few of influence, wealth, and note remaining. What attitude would they assume? What, in short, was the extent, the core, the nature of the crisis? Was there or was there not a general concert of all peoples, tribes, religions, and dialects for the expulsion of the British? Were the forty-three independent potentates all linked in the hideous confederacy? Was it a national and continental rebellion? Was an angry and suffering people struggling for liberty?

The predicament was one in which the greatest boldness was the greatest prudence. The time for action, not inquiry, had come. There was a violent public and political reaction to apprehend, a certain failure of revenue to contend against, a commercial paralysis to avert, mutiny at home to look to, a future famine in Hindoostan almost inevitable, reinforcements before Delhi to be provided. All communication with Calcutta had been totally and completely cut off.

The following pages will show how just was the confidence placed in the loyalty and honour of the chieftains of Puttiala, of Jheend, and of Bikaneer. The aim with which they have been written is to depict how the Punjab Government, fortified by the moral and physical support of its noble and loyal allies, and assured of the attachment of its people, embarked on a series of operations based on one broad grand line of policy; which, whether for the almost desperate nerve that maintained it through four toiling months, or the success which triumphantly crowned it, must for ever remain to the world a monument of wisdom and self-denying heroism: but that wisdom and that heroism are still but mere dross before the manifest and wondrous interposition of Almighty God in the cause of Christianity.

CONTENTS.

CHAPTER I.

CHAPTER II.

CHAPTER III.

CHAPTER IV.

CHAPTER V.

CHAPTER IX.

THE CRISIS IN THE PUNJAB.

CHAPTER I.

DISARMING OF THE NATIVE TROOPS AT MEEAN MEER ON THE THIRTEENTH OF MAY, AND MUTINY ON THE SAME DAY AT FEROZEPORE.

MEEAN MEER is the large military cantonment situated five or six miles from Lahore. On the 13th of May, the European, or reliable, troops consisted of H. M.'s 81st, about 850 strong, and two troops of horse artillery, H.E.I.C.S., also European. The doubtful were composed of the 16th Grenadier N. I., famous for service in Mysore, Seringapatam, Afghanistan, Guznee, Candahar, Cabool, Maharajpoor, Moodkee, Ferozshuhur, Subraon, with embroidered Star for Seringapatam on its colours, and a Royal Tiger under Banian Tree for Mysore. The 26th (Light) N. I. (since annihilated), which had served with distinction in Arracan, Cabul (1842) Moodkee, Ferozshuhur, Subraon; and the 49th, which had served at Arracan, Punjab, and Mooltan. Also the 8th Regiment Light Cavalry, with "Bhurtpoor," "Puniar," "Maharajpoor," "Ferozshuhur," "Punjab," "Chillianwallah," "Goojerat," as evidence of its former achievements.

On the 12th May, the shadow of coming events had not cast its gloom over society: a ball and supper was to be given on that evening. While the ordinary preparations for this festivity were in process, extraordinary measures for a very different spectacle for the morning were being matured.

Intelligence of the Meerut outbreak reached Lahore on the 11th; on the morning of the 12th of May a hurried telegram told the deeds at Delhi. The Chief Commissioner was in the north at Rawul Pindee. His mantle was on the shoulders of Robert Montgomery, the Judicial Commissioner, who at a glance saw that the imminency admitted of no delay. He accordingly summoned forthwith a conference of the leading officers of the civil station at Anarkullee, viz., Mr. Donald Mc Leod, Financial Commissioner; Mr. A. A. Roberts, Commissioner; Major Ommanney, Chief Engineer; Col. Macpherson, Military Secretary; Capt. Lawrence, and Capt. Hutchinson,

The proposition of the Judicial Commissioner, that Brigadier Stuart Corbett, commanding at

Meean Meer, should be moved to deprive the native corps of their ammunition, was unanimously acquiesced in.

Accordingly, accompanied by Colonel Macpherson, Mr. Montgomery proceeded to Meean Meer, and suggested the plan to Brigadier Corbett, who agreed. Subsequently, in the afternoon, further disaster was telegraphed from Delhi, and the Brigadier resolved on the grand and original move of depriving the sepoy of his arms altogether.

The ball was permitted to proceed; but it soon languished: strange rumours got about the room concerning the morning parade of all troops, which had been announced for daybreak.

Scarcely before the dancers had departed, three Companies of H. M.'s 81st fell in and marched off to the fort at Lahore under Colonol Smith. Ten men per company had been also ordered to sleep in their barrack-rooms with "their clothes on." At four o'clock in the morning, the remainder of the regiment fell in, and were ordered "to loosen their ammunition;" a proceeding which aroused the curiosity of the honest soldiers to the highest pitch. Knowing looks began to be exchanged, and queries to the purport of "What's in the wind" were freely passed, but not responded to, as none could divine.

Leaving the barrack guards doubled, six companies, twenty-four files each, started for the parade ground, and were formed up in contiguous columns. The position of the troops at this sunrise parade was as follows:—

PRELIMINARY FORMATION.

8th Cavalry, Native.	*49th N.I.*	*26th N.I.*	*16th N.I.*	*H.M.'s 81st.*	*H. E. I. C. H. A.*
....	...	...	...	...	† † † † † †
....	...	...	...	...	
....	...	...	...	...	† † † † † †
....	...	...	...	...	
....	...	...	...	...	
	...	...	...	...	
	...	...	...	...	
	...	...	...	...	

As the enormous mass of Indian soldiery swept past the small but deeply interested band of spectators from Anarkullee, one absorbing thought occupied all bosoms—"Are their muskets already loaded?" The suspense though short was painful.

The Brigadier having directed to be read out, at the head of each regiment, the Governor-General's order on the disbanding of the 34th N. I. at Barrackpore, he himself, a Colonel of the 16th Grenadiers, commenced by addressing the senior regiment: he complimented all, seriatim, on the distinguished reputation they had borne hitherto, and intimated dimly the step which it was his painful duty now to adopt. Quick as thought the word passed. The native regiments changed front to the rear, by the wheel of sub-divisions round the centre, while at the same time the artillery (quietly loading as they moved, unobserved by the sepoys), and her Majesty's 81st, about three hundred altogether, formed line facing the native regiments. A ringing rattle at the same time announced that the Queen's corps had also loaded. Nothing could be more soldierly than their tramp—more menacing than their front.

For the benefit of the unmilitary reader, a supplementary sketch is now offered, and his imagination may conceive the countenances of the sepoys when they received the order to pile arms. The artillery port-fires were also lighted, and the guns ready to belch forth grape into every regiment.

SECOND FORMATION.

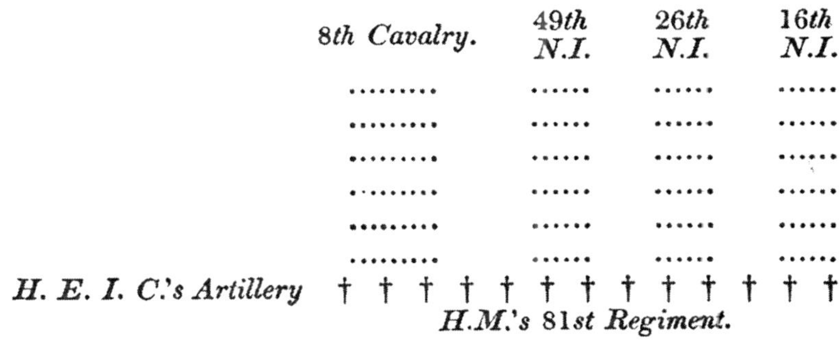

Hesitation was useless. The sepoys confronted immediate death: in which, by the way, the officers would have been sacrificed. Some say their demeanour varied, and that the 16th Grenadiers made a clutch at their arms when they appreciated their utter discomfiture. Be this as it may, the regiments, shorn of their arms, marched back; the bands playing and colours flying. A company of her Majesty's 81st fell out, in ordinary course; and with the cool complacency of the European who summed up the whole crisis with the question to his commanding officer—"I suppose, sir, it's them niggers again," they, in an orderly and business-like way, packed the weapons of the dishonoured soldiery in carts, and escorted them to barracks.

This refreshing spectacle thus concluded; and it was the first of the sort. Simple as was the affair, common-place apparently as was the manœuvre, the transaction of that morning hour was the turning point in the destiny of the Punjab. The Asiatic mind, "unstable as water," had been dealt with in the mode that has ever insured success. The "initiative" had been taken, and the tables turned on him: trumps were led while he was finessing. Some 3,500 men, with treachery and rebellion at their hearts, their plans concerted, but their aim uncertain, quietly laid down their arms in the presence of a dozen guns and three hundred rank and file of H.M.'s 81st Regiment. It was, in a military point of view, a simple, peaceful, and, politically speaking, a fateful piece of business. All honour to those who carried out the operation.

The momentous value of the step was not long coming to light. Expresses had been despatched to all stations announcing the measures. Tremblers stood aghast at its boldness; some military men questioned the sanity of the originators; but ere three days were over all admitted the foresight and wisdom displayed. No man now looked into the countenance of a sepoy without scanning it. The non-observance of ordinary salutation began to be noticed. The mist gradually fell from before men's eyes.

God put it into the hearts of our rulers to act with such energy and resolution. It came to their knowledge, from intercepted correspondence, that the whole mine of revolt had been laid with deep and wary cunning. On the very morning of the 13th, the fort at Lahore was to have been relieved. The relief on its arrival would have doubled the ordinary strength of the native garrison; making it about 1,000 or, 1,200 men. The scheme they had in contemplation was to rush upon and overcome the small party of Europeans; seize the fort, the extensive magazines, the armoury, the vast treasure; whilst the remaining regiments were to rise and massacre all the Europeans of Meean Meer and Anarkullee, and release the prisoners incarcerated in the central gaol, some two thousand in number!

That the capital was saved is due (under God) to the promptitude of the measures adopted; and events at Ferozepore six hours after, vindicated the wisdom of the acts of Government.

The *coup de grace* had scarcely been given at Lahore, when, on the same day, the 45th N. I., which had served at Moodkee, Ferozshuhur, Punjab, Chillianwalla, and Goojerat, showed their true colours.

A deep-set plot must have been laid between the regiments of Meean Meer and Ferozepore. At this latter place the magazine contained enormous military stores; and had these gone, the British flag would not now have been waving over the walls of Delhi. Brigadier Innes was fully aware of the immense value of the arsenal. Notwithstanding the confidence professed, perhaps naturally, by officers commanding the N. I. corps, a haughty manner was evident among the native soldiery on the parade of the morning of the 13th. Cæsar's wife, as usual, was to be above suspicion, and from this reasoning it was "hoped" the 45th and 57th N. I. would be found "satisfactory."

Again the initiative was adopted; though perhaps hardly to a sufficient extent. On receipt of the Delhi news the native troops were quietly moved out of cantonments, and the entrenchments occupied by a detachment of H.M.'s 61st under Major Redmond. Twelve guns also proceeded thither. The 45th at once broke out into open mutiny; and, filled with the hope of yet carrying out the design in which they now felt they had been frustrated, they rushed with escalading ladders to the entrenchments. These ladders must have been provided by them long before. Major Redmond's company repulsed the whole regiment; unfortunately he was badly wounded. The magazine was saved; but the 45th roamed about in bodies, and burned some ten or sixteen buildings, including the church and the Roman Catholic chapel. H. M.'s 61st lost the messhouse and all their property. Again and again fruitless attempts were made on the entrenchments by the mutineers. To ensure safety, the magazines of the N. I. regiments had been blown up.

Foiled in their concerted plan, when disunited, the 45th, like the unstrung bundle of faggots, became separately frangible. Some two hundred and more broke away into small parties. They flung arms and colours into a well, and were hunted up, exhausted and famished, in the various independent states. About one half remained. The pursuit was so sharp that had they remained in a body, and had the 10th Light Cavalry proved staunch, as they seemed to be then, the 45th must have been annihilated. The 57th N.I. laid down their arms at request; but with a defiant air, significant of the feelings with which they had been animated, and the disappointment they felt. The want of that perfect sympathy and cordial co-operation, which mark the attitude of those who have some great common cause at heart, was never more shown than in the demeanour of the 10th Light Cavalry, who have all mutinied since. When lukewarmness, not to say opposition, might have been dangerous, they remained steady under the moral hold of their officers.

Some accounts state that shades of guilt were attempted to be drawn between the 57th and 45th N. I. All that is certain is that the disbandment of the former regiment came too late. The regiment had anticipated their fate. The following order was read out to some half-dozen remnants.

"Sepoys of the '*Lord Moira-ke-pultun*', (57th N. I.) listen to the order of the Commander-in-Chief *Sahib Bahadoor:* he has ordered you to be disbanded; the reasons are these:—Before a Court of Inquiry it has been proved that you would not receive the new Enfield rifles; your replies to the Court were evasive. Now, these rifles differ very little from the muskets which you have hitherto been using, and your forefathers for the last century before you. This refusal to receive the new weapon on the alleged plea that you would lose your caste, is but an artifice to conceal your real intentions, which are nothing else than to revolt against the Government, which feeds you now, and pensions you when you become superannuated. On the 13th May, when the *Murreeroo-ke-pultun* (45th N. I.) mutinied, and attempted to seize the entrenched magazine, a company of your regiment was on duty there, and, instead of firing on the mutineers, they loaded their muskets to destroy the European soldiers, whom the Brigadier Commanding had then sent to protect the magazine. Subsequently some 300 sepoys deserted, and the guard of your regiment on duty in the district, excited the people there to join with them in making a religious war against the British. Such has been the conduct of the *Lord Moira-ke-pultun.* Now, hear your punishment—your colours shall be furled—your number effaced out of the army list, and yourselves deported under proper escort to your homes."

Before the final desertion, even of men selected for their previous good character, the Judicial Commissioner, on his own responsibility, had urged that the remainder should be marched to gaol, and shot to a man, in case of the slightest opposition.

And yet so contradictory and anomalous were appearances, that the demeanour of the 45th N. I., perhaps greater adepts in duplicity, inspired the greater confidence.

The 57th were never allowed to be in a position in which they could, on the day and night of the 13th, be called upon to act either with or against the 45th N. I. Hence when the 45th openly mutinied, expecting aid from the 57th, the latter did all that was required—they remained quiet. The outbreak of the 45th was as sudden and as little expected as the outbreak at Meerut; but timely precaution saved the station from the tragedies of Meerut. No murders darkened the homes of Ferozepore; though the havoc and riot for a time was scarcely inferior to that of the last-mentioned station.

Had there not been some twenty thousand barrels of gunpowder to care for in the arsenal, the churches and the houses would not, perhaps, have been sacrificed. The safety of the former was not dearly purchased by the ignominious discomfiture of the mutinous corps. Had the two corps been in a position at any moment to unite, the 10th Light Cavalry would, as events have proved, have been unable to resist temptation; and the thatched barracks would have had to be defended, and the magazine left. The fort, so called, could be entered at all points: a spark would have ignited the magazine, and blown all living into eternity. It was no fault of the mutineers that this did not occur. Three hundred of the 57th N. I. deserted in the hour of trial, and the rest remained with their officers, who could not but distrust them.

On the 28th of May, the remainder of the 45th were turned ingloriously out of cantonments, and escorted to the boundaries of the district. They probably combated with no diminished acrimony against us at Delhi from having been allowed to reach it alive without money and without food. Nothing in the shape of vile or insidious reports, here or elsewhere, had been omitted that could inflame the bazaar people. Slaughtered cows and pigs, it was confidently affirmed, had been thrown into wells so as to *kharáb kur*, or ruin the faiths of all sects, whether Hindoo, Sikh, or Mahomedan. Moulvies preached insurrection in the streets and the mosques. But their ministry was of short duration, under the vigilant Major Marsden.

General Van Cortlandt, of Mooltan and Bunnoo celebrity, had been wisely selected by the Chief Commissioner to raise and organize irregulars. Under his influence the work proceeded apace, and he was soon in a position to enter upon his work, and to take formal command. The services rendered by this well-known and veteran officer, in conjunction with those of Captain Pearse, Messrs. Oliver and Macdonald, do not properly find scope in the present work, which professes only to notice the events of the Punjab. But a short summary of them may not be uninteresting:—

On the principle *ne quid detrimenti capiat* the Punjab Government undertook immediately the re-organization of the North-Western provinces of Sirsa, Hansi, and Hissar, although a month previous they had been as little under their control as Oudh itself.

A force was arranged and despatched, the only Europeans being the officers! The success was gradual, but complete; a sufficient proof of the impression existing on the general mind of the invincibility of the British Government, and the security and the stability of its institutions. The almost instantaneous occupation of these provinces in such dangerous proximity to the focus of rebellion, was fraught with value to our cause. The blow was struck before delay had sapped our prestige.

The troops of Brigadier-General Van Cortlandt were all Irregulars. About 300 Dogras were at first the nucleus of his force, belonging to Rajah Jowahir Singh; whose troops, in the midst of the city of Lahore, were thus adroitly made use of. Since then the Dogras (a short built, sturdy race) have amounted to about one thousand men in rank and file. Two hundred disciplined "Kutar Mookhies" of Tronson's Mooltan Regiment were added, also about one hundred of the police sowars belonging to the same gallant officer. They accompanied Captain Pearse from Googaira. Add to this a couple of guns and a regiment of raw levies raised by himself, some few Peshawuree sowars, and a small detachment of Patiala horse and foot, and the reader has the sum of the whole force, which was the first to throw down the gauntlet in the cause of law and order. Some aid also arrived from the Bikaneer Rajah; but, as the composition of it seemed "of questionable material," the services of this contingent were courteously dispensed with.

Nerved by the stimulating hope of being the instruments of wreaking just vengeance on the authors of the massacres, the officers were prepared to view mournful relics of harrowing fates, and they felt at least a mournful solace to their bitter feelings in performing the last rites to such few remnants of human English remains as wild dogs and decomposition had permitted to remain above ground to bleach in the scorching sun. The bodies of Captain Hilliard and Mr. Fell, which, after their base murder, had been flung into a well, were taken reverently out and interred with honour within sacred precincts. Other dreadful evidences of massacre were discovered.

When force was necessary, or when conciliation and pacification were expedient, Van Cortlandt employed both, and invariably with effect. Almost immediately on his arrival he gained a decisive victory over the rebel Bhuttees, with the slightest possible loss, on the 19th of June, when he routed the enemy from a strong position. They numbered some two thousand, of whom two hundred fell on the field of action.

Sirsa, depopulated, half sacked and half burnt, the tombs of the Christians and the little cemetery half despoiled, owes its regeneration to the strong courage and fortitude of Mr. Oliver; who had never left his post, and never lost his self-possession, though within sight and earshot of death and the sounds of death. His perfect reliance in the immediate succour he so effectually received was rewarded, and he was soon engaged in restoring that confidence which overpowering numbers only for a time had been enabled to shake, and in establishing the power of the British Government on a surer and firmer basis than before.

We have not space for details of the various measures adopted; and, therefore, only proceed to record a brilliant achievement, early in September, of Lieutenant Pearse, who commanded the cavalry attached to the Bhuttianah Field Force under Brigadier Van Cortlandt.

A pensioned subadar, one of the chief instigators of the mutiny in the Hurrianah Light Infantry Battalion, had found refuge in a rebel Ranghur village called Bitoul. Lieutenant Pearse, accompanied by Mr. Ford, C.S., and Mr. Kitchen, his clerk, with 280 horse, and some few Peshawurees and Bikaneers, marched to the village through a country inundated with rain, and found its position strong, and the garrison strong. The eastern gate was thought weak, but on a rush at it being made, it proved much stronger than expected. The wood work could not be fired from the wet. Lieutenant Pearse dismounted; battered it down with his gallant Peshawurees, killed the miscreant Goor Buksh, the pensioner, with many others, and sacked the entire place. Not a woman, however, was allowed to be touched. No such stain has yet dimmed the lustre of British triumphs.

Again on the 11th of September, General Van Cortlandt, with Lieutenants Sadlier and Hunt, attacked and destroyed another rebel village of Mungolee. The slaughter of the rebels and mutineers spread terror among the disaffected throughout the whole district. Such was the consternation among the insurgents, that on the 13th they fled on the approach of Van Cortlandt's force, after firing half a day ineffectual shots at a most cautious distance.

A few more villages have been thus condignly punished, and tranquillity completely restored. The army was entirely Asiatic, but commanded by a few officers of established repute, and aided by the presence of amateurs of all classes, who have been repeatedly thanked for their aid in meting out swift and merited retribution.

CHAPTER II.

GENERAL MEASURES ADOPTED AT LAHORE AND UMRITSUR—MARCH OF THE ARMY TO DELHI.

THE immediate crisis having been averted by the proceedings sketched in the foregoing Chapter, Mr. Montgomery promptly turned his attention to internal politics. Public confidence was to be maintained, excitement was to be appeased, and messages flashed incessantly to and fro, directing, warning, and counselling. All day and all night express horsemen galloped from one station to another. The city of Lahore, filled with Mahomedans, was fully alive to the state of things. Every look and gesture of those in authority was keenly eyed. Death had removed in Rajah Deena Nath a palpable thorn in our side. But there were still enough left to elicit the utmost diplomatic address. The urgency of the situation had to be explained frankly, while the hope of the eventual triumph, under Providence, had to take the garb of human certainty. The present contingency was admitted to be unforeseen, unmerited, and such has as yet beset no ordinary throne since empires were. It was one marked by such baseness and ingratitude that the fidelity of honourable men could safely be calculated upon in actively expressing their abhorrence.

Equally dangerous would have been any show of disaffection in the sister and neighbouring capital of Umritsur. Vast commercial interests were involved in its safety; within its walls, too, are enshrined the essence of the mystery, and the relics of the traditionary epochs of the Sikh national faith. The population, swelled by the sudden stoppage of the current of traffic from the north, must have increased to nearly one hundred and fifty thousand souls. Every class, creed, grade, and clime of Asia, were represented. The trade operations were intimately mixed up with Delhi; and the great commission brokers and capitalists, who never thought of politics beyond how it affected the money market, and who had always steadily backed the irresistible "ekbal" of the Government, experienced a rude shock when it was announced that the Grand Trunk Road was (for the first time since the British rule) impassable. The temporary suspension of trade afforded leisure for surmise, and the discussion of politics became the order of the day. It is impossible to say to what pitch the agitation amongst the burghers might not have arisen, but for the wonderful peace kept throughout those troublous days in Bombay and Scinde, the roads through which were always safe. Not only was physical support and reinforcement afforded to the Punjab by the indefatigable efforts of Lord Elphinstone and Mr. Frere, but the most advantageous moral impression was kept up, by the entire tranquillity and freedom of intercourse which they contrived, in the teeth of stupendous difficulties, to preserve intact.

It remained to be seen whether the poisonous matter, which had for the first time produced temporary cohesion and unity of action among Hindoos and Mahomedans, would be absorbed into the Sikh system. But notwithstanding the thriving mission school and church close abutting on the holy tank and temple, so marked had been the principle of religious toleration, and so perfectly appreciated, that from first to last no symptom of wavering has betrayed itself. Much to the contrary, even; for the conduct of the mutinous traitors has evoked national condemnation, while the atrocities upon the helpless evoked national commiseration. The steadiness of the atmosphere at Umritsur, lent almost unhoped for weight to the public cause.

To return to the immediate measures adopted. All conventional formalism was banished by Mr. Montgomery. His instructions sped swiftly throughout the country, and before the sepoys had time to recover from the blows at Meean Meer and Ferozepore, and ten days after at Peshawur, all outlying treasure had been brought under proper custody and temptation thereby removed. All letters had been way-laid; the Hindoostanee element in the executive and detective force gradually fell into disuse; the cupidity of the villagers was excited by rich rewards for the capture of mutinous sepoys dead or alive; the great forts of Lahore and Govindghur had been abundantly stored; measures in all directions had been adopted against surprise, and the gaol guards were added to. Meanwhile the ordinary courts suspended not their functions, but the civil and criminal business was carried on with as much apparent calmness as if the most common-place occurrences of tranquil government existence were taking place, and the flames of rebellion were not lapping up province after province in Hindoostan.

Emissaries of every garb and hue had been despatched by the indefatigable machinators to undermine the Sikhs and upset the tottering loyalty of the Native Infantry corps in the Punjab—the latter but too successfully. A vast accession of Byragee faqueers, it was remarked, had cropped out. Political arrests became rapid. The haunts of old Sikh fanatics were looked up, and their inmates cared for. Curiously-bedizened men affected to walk about Suddur stations with an unusual partiality for swords and matchlocks. They were all arrested, their arms seized, and securities taken from them if their answers were satisfactory; otherwise they were imprisoned *sine die, i. e.*, pending the upshot of events.

Offers of aid and service poured in immediately on the Government; but it was not politic to appear as if we threw ourselves upon the people; so with expressions of thanks, and promises to indent upon their active allegiance should necessity arise, the sirdars and chiefs were deceived as to the magnitude of the crisis, and the extent of their own power. Impassible as the countenance of Louis Napoleon, was the aspect worn by the local Government. Such calmness was the more necessary as the alarm among the European residents deepened in intensity.

Thus no half-measures were adopted. Moreover, the principle that he who is not for us is against us was strictly followed. There was no pause. Treason and sedition were dogged into the very privacy of the harem, and up to the sacred sanctuaries of mosques and shrines. Learned moulvies were seized in the midst of a crowd of fanatic worshippers, and men of distinction and note were "wanted" at dead of night. Like sleugh-hounds, the district police, on the first scent of treason, and egged on by the certainty of reward, fastened on the track, and left it not until the astonished intriguer was grounded in his lair. As with the detectives of Vidocq, there were spies in the market-place, at the festival, in the places of worship, in the gaols, in the hospitals, in the regimental bazaars, among the casual knot of gossippers on the bridge, among the bathers at the tanks, among the village circle round the well under the big tree, among the pettifogging hangers-on of the courts, among the stone-breakers of the highways, among the dusty travellers at the serais. No man's tongue was his own property. Asiatic chicane was paralysed before the newly-aroused volition of the Anglo-Saxon.

The determination and unflagging activity of the authorities incited the Sikhs to emulation. At the Mustee Gate of Lahore one day, a man said to be a Hindoostanee, entered, wearing a sword; he was challenged, and, replying vaguely, was stopped. He cut down the sentry, and made off; he was pursued, fired at, and dropped on the banks of the Ravee: the ball had divided an artery. He died and made no sign, and was never recognised. Swift his doom. But what was the errand of this desperate wretch? That must lie hidden until the secrets of all hearts are open.

Gradually, as the rivers rose, all ferries were closely watched, and breast-works erected at the ghâts, by order of Sir John Lawrence.

Intelligence was received express from Lahore, at seven o'clock in the evening of the 14th May, at Umritsur, that the disarmed regiments of Meean Meer were meditating flight, possibly towards Ferozepore; but it was thought more likely that they would attempt to swarm into Govindghur, once the asylum of the far-famed Koh-i-noor; as at that time it contained but a weak company of artillery, under Captain H. B. Macleod, the majority of the garrison being composed of no less than 216 armed Poorbeah soldiery.

Within one hour from the receipt of the intelligence, the battery of artillery from the cantonment, under Captain Waddy, was moved for safety into the fort—horses and all,—the manœuvre being as steadily and swiftly performed as if on ordinary inspection parade; a portion of the 59th N. I. (since disarmed) were picquetted out in various directions, as if they were the most staunch and trusty followers, to stop the entry of the mutineers; and a picquet of sowars and Sikhs, under the Deputy-Commissioner, were located just opposite the fort gates, in order to charge in upon a preconcerted signal. It was an anxious and sleepless night for all; but it passed off quietly, as the alarm was a false one, and the opportunity was lost never to return.

An agreeable instance of the sort of reception which the Poorbeah sepoy was likely to meet with at the hands of the sturdy Punjabee Jats was shown on that day. Mr. Macnaghten, Assistant-Commissioner, volunteered to go out half-way to Lahore and raise a human barrier of villagers across the road to intercept the rebels. The enthusiasm displayed by the country people sufficiently proved that they were "non-conductors" of rebellion. One valiant rustic, armed only with a spade, brought in a tall man, whom he swore was a Hindoostanee, and requested orders as to his disposal, with the implement in his hand. Providence had blessed the Punjab with a golden harvest, such as had not been known for many long years, and the country was too happy and prosperous to join in any *emeute,* out of pure friendship to their hereditary enemies. Dewan Narain Singh and Sirdar Khan Singh, of Ataree, were eager to aid, and their conduct contrasted with that of a Sirdar Nahr Singh, who was asleep, "and could not be disturbed" when sent for by the Assistant-Commissioner, and who became suddenly afflicted with a "boil" of an alarming nature on a distressing segment of his person!

About midnight, Mr. Macnaghten, hearing a great tramp, as of the coming rebels, mustered all his villagers, drew carts across the road (some villagers suggesting that the oxen and bullocks should remain, as the Hindoos wouldn't cut through them), and awaited the attack. The noise was that of forty "ekkas," containing about eighty gallant soldiers, under Lieut. Chichester, of H. M.'s 81st, who, seeing the barrier dimly through the darkness, drew his revolver. The *denouement* of the anticipated drama was gratifying on both sides. Next morning the rustic soldiery returned to their homes.

As yet this fine population, composing the Manjha, the nursery of the Khalsa soldiery, have not only escaped contagion, but have contributed their glorious old artillerymen who did such execution at Ferozshuhur and Moodkee, in a cause which was honourable because national.*

* The solicitude of the Judicial Commissioner for the safety and welfare of Govindghur and Umritsur may be gathered

A new vein of cases was opened out in the criminal courts as soon as the correspondence from Hindoostan came to be intercepted. The extent and

from the accompanying appalling letter, dated the 12th of May. It was received the very morning of the arrival of the news of the outbreak. It was the first intimation which arrived, and was written the day before the disarming at Lahore.

"*Lahore, May 12th*, 1857.

"MY DEAR COOPER,—You may not have heard, as you have no electric telegraph station, that the troops at Meerut and Delhi have risen, and the Europeans are defending their lives as well as they can—as yet it is not known with what results. But the city of Delhi is in a very excited state, and the communication between Delhi and Meerut is cut off. It is expected that the troops at Umballah, who have shown great disaffection, will rise, and we must expect the rebellion to spread. The native troops here are not well affected, and we may have to fight for our lives. My object is to write and put you on your guard. Communicate with the commanding officer. Care for Govindghur, and it may be necessary to remove the sepoys from there. It would be the place of general resort should unhappily such a necessity arise. I would advise every precaution being adopted beforehand, so as to be ready in case of a row. You shall have the best information of all that is going on, and the more quietly we move the better. Do not alarm the sepoys by any previous acts, but keep the strictest watch on them, and the feelings of the city should be ascertained by every source at your command. Open communication with Jullundur, and find out what is going on there. My advice, then, is to be fully alive, and awake and prepared for the worst, without creating any alarm by any open act. If the troops should rise, you have the fort to go to, and can defend yourselves. Let me or Roberts hear constantly as to the feeling of all troops, people, &c., &c.

"Believe me, yours truly,

"Fred. Cooper, Esq. ROBERT MONTGOMERY."

intricacy of the web woven for the entanglement of the Government soon appeared. To undermine the Sikh loyalty, a buniah wrote from Jugadaree that the price of wheat was unprecedently low, and all were in excellent spirits, until it was found that Government had mixed *pulverised bones with the flour.* A Sikh sepoy, moreover, in an intercepted note, confided his views of the politics of the day to a friend, saying that personally he was indifferent under the circumstances, but there was a great uproar; the Feringhees, he feared, could not last long: they were being beaten over and over again before Delhi. But he didn't know what monarchy would supplant them exactly. At Jhelum, the Deputy-Commissioner opened a letter containing a plot for the massacre of the whole of a British family at Julundur. At Peshawur, a naick of the 64th N. I. was hanged for receiving a letter (obviously a reply to a query as to the disposal of the Europeans.) "*They were to be all massacred, without respect to age, sex, or person.*" An intercepted letter, however, from an old subahdar of the 21st N. I. (still armed), also obviously in reply, urged the sepoys to stand by their salt, as, though the mutineers might have their way for three months, after that the British would be supreme again. And this fine corps possessed the proud but melancholy distinction of being the only regiment of the line wholly armed.

Allegoric and symbolic commerce also commenced. "Pearls," that is white faces, were quoted low in the market; and "red wheat," Hindoostan, looking up. A letter from Monghyr, of the 26th of May, contained the following passage literally translated:—"The state of affairs is this:—Dost Mahomed Khan, Ghazee, has marched from Cabul and come to see Sir John Lawrence. He declares that the Emperor of Russia and the Shah of Herat have met, with the intention of invading Hindoostan. Dost Mahomed Khan has come to Sir John Lawrence for this reason, that the army of the empire is very numerous, though the number is not yet known. But if any one could count the number of the soldiers having seen an ant hill, what could be more numerous?"

Another intercepted letter early in the crisis intimated to a brother in the native artillery that the Government army was assembling at Kurnaul, and requested a reply as to the exact date of the recipients' mutiny and march for co-operation with the rebels. An old subahdar of artillery also had been so prepossessed with the notion of the frailty of the tenure of the Government, that though nearly blind and deaf, and unfit for active service, he was ready to do anything to secure an appointment under the new '*Raj*.'" There was no lack of *gobemouches* throughout the army.

The Sikhs generally were most eager to aid in the capture of Delhi, from the existence of a most remarkable prophecy,—that they, in conjunction with "*topee wallahs*" (hat wearers, or the British), who should come over the sea, would reconquer Delhi, and place the head of the king's son on the very spot where the head of Gooroo Teg Bahadoor had been exposed, one hundred and eighty years before, by order of Aurungzebe, the Great Mogul. This vaticination was almost literally carried out, for when the gallant Hodson had captured the old king and shot the two sons, his Sikh ressaldar, diligently remembering the oracle, secured its fulfilment; and for three days, on the spot foretold, the bodies of the king's sons lay a spectacle to men; the glazed eyes of these miscreants staring sternly out of their dead heads on the very scene where they had ordered and witnessed the massacre of the English women and children. But to resume.

Soon after the outbreak, a Hindoostanee walked into the Government school at Umritsur, and mentioned casually, in conversation to the moulvies, that the King of Delhi had intimated, in writing, to Mr. Montgomery, at Lahore, that he was indebted to him for his excellent arrangements hitherto on his behalf for the affairs of India; but that he could now dispense with his services, as he himself was prepared to undertake the necessary arrangements for the future government of India; and that he now accorded his royal permission to that gentleman to retire, *viâ* Bombay. A Mussulman city watchman tried the mettle of the local authorities by wounding a cow in the streets. He was at once publicly flogged with the utmost severity, and imprisoned for a year, with labour and irons. Nothing of the kind has occurred since. Native Christians had been threatened in the streets: Paulus, a convert, was informed that "his ears would shortly be pulled."

The shops of the Elahee and Nubbee Bukshes, as familiar in India as Moses and Son in England, who had battened and thrived upon the Europeans' addiction to the "secondary wants,"—beer, brandy, pickles, hams, wines, cigars, &c., not produceable in India—became the arenas of political discussion. The Delhi, Bareilly, and Shajehanpore massacres were freely canvassed, and the necessity of imitation became a matter of common-place talk. The admixture of cows'-bones was accepted as a fact, and the Sikhs were instigated to make it a *casus belli.* But the Reverend "Daood," David, an ordained (Sikh) clergyman, would never leave his post in the city from first to last, and always gave out that hereafter for tens there would be thousands of converts. A man, Noor Mahomed Khan, had absolutely ridden from Delhi, since the massacre, to inaugurate the "Crusade." He was lately Serishtadar of the Canals, and in his bundle were seen suits of fakeers' clothes, and disguises for future emergencies! He was all but speechless on being arrested, and his physiognomy a picture of what imagination gives to the butchers of Delhi. All these well-wishers have died a hundred deaths since; for from that day until this they have been in solitary confinement, waiting, perhaps, to hear the joyful sound of a riot in the gaol, such as in Hindoostan greeted the ears of almost every prisoner.

Thus the character of the insurrection had soon developed itself. Had all the suspected been pursued, the number of Mussulmen involved would have become embarrassing to Government. So this new danger had to be avoided; and until power is again physically as well as morally substantial (as it ought to be) instead of too shadowy, as it was when the insurrection broke out, Islamism will not feel its degradation in India.

But even larger matters were absorbing the attention of Government. The state of affairs close upon the borders of these Provinces, that would arise after the outbreak of the Hurrianah Local Battalion and the dismal tragedies of Hansi and Hissar, with the inevitable disorganization consequent thereon, was a source of peculiar anxiety. The native princes were called upon to aid in the preservation of law and order, and, with the exception of the Jhujjur Chief (since hanged for high treason), who was at least lukewarm, the demand was cordially responded to. The efforts of their Highnesses of Patiala, and Bikaneer, and Kuppoorthullah, will ever stand forth in history as noble instances of Asiatic honour under circumstances of unparalleled temptation. Considerations of common-sense and pride; the first, inasmuch as possession of Company's paper dictated prudence; the second, because they could, at the utmost, but play second and third fiddle to the Great Mogul (he being then actually a dependent pensioner, while they were virtually independent rulers), no doubt had their share in the process of ratiocination. Still all had their own fancied or real wrongs to urge; and be it said in vindication of their delicacy, they did not select the season of embarrassment either to expatiate on them, or to extract promises.

The Umballa district in the months of May and June attracted all eyes. The late Commander-in-Chief was there awaiting the arrival of indispensable equipments in the siege train from Philour. Fire after fire was occurring continually, and no punishment was meted out. The native regiments continued doggedly sulky. The Judicial Commissioner had telegraphed as follows to the Commander-in-Chief, but without effect*:—

"Intelligence from Ferozepoor.—About 400 of the 45th with arms have got off to Fureedkote. Sirdars called in to capture them. The disarmed mutineers at Ferozepoor sulky. Brigadier Innes has been asked to march them to the Civil Gaol, and destroy them if they resist. Unless you think that the 60th, 25th, and 5th have so far committed themselves as to justify condign punishment, I earnestly suggest that you at least disarm and confine them in the Civil Gaol, which Mr. Barnes will empty on your showing this. The civil authorities will take charge of the men, and you will be relieved from anxiety."

The advice was not followed. But the Commander-

* From the first, Montgomery had felt that timely severity was the greatest humanity in the end; and that to prevent bloodshed, the sword must be wrested from the murderer's hands at all present sacrifice.

in-Chief telegraphed to Lahore to learn how the disarming had been effected there!

Meanwhile all available Europeans were streaming down from the hill stations of Kussowlie and Dugshai; their departure, as will be seen hereafter, not adding to the restoration of comfort among the numerous residents. To add to the unexampled embarrassments of a Commander-in-Chief, a wing of the 60th N. I. was warned to be ready to march, but with infamous insolence the regiment refused, unless all were ordered to go! Perhaps General Anson then began to regret his unpopularity with the Native army, and in the humiliating concessions he had now to make, almost under coercion, bethought himself of having given out a few short months previously, when the cartridge agitation was rife and menacing, that he "would never give in to their beastly prejudices!"

Two companies of the 5th N. I., on duty at Thanusur (the neighbouring station), had shown signs of open mutiny; but the ever ready Patiala chieftain detached a force to keep the main line open from thence to Kurnaul. In the language of his own vakeel he seemed to sleep with one eye open to the interests of the British army. Nay, more, he sheltered and entertained with princely hospitality the famished and scorched fugitives who escaped the massacres of Hansi and Hissar. Altogether the physical contingent this noble ally supplied must have been about what Sardinia afforded the allies in the Crimea; but the moral influence of the aid furnished cannot be measured in the same way. The British Parliament will know how to requite such generous and gratuitous service.

An immediate advance would have been imperative had adequate force been present; and much captious and hasty criticism was elicited by the delay. Meanwhile, the mutineers at Delhi were erecting a series of most formidable entrenchments, behind which they determinately gave, but soon lost, the first and gloriously decisive battle before its walls. No Commander-in-Chief was ever placed in such a predicament before. If the policy was Fabian, it was Fabian on compulsion. Until the Punjab reinforcements arrived, the head of the army had absolutely no force reliable but the Europeans.

The actual advance will be seen from the annexed extract from the *Lahore Chronicle*, dated the 26th of May, or fifteen days after the outbreak:—

"We arrived here yesterday morning, 3 A.M. Six companies 1st Bengal Fusiliers, and one squadron H. M.'s 9th Lancers. The Chief and Staff arrived during the day. We march again this evening to

Paneeput, 20 miles. The force that marched from this on our arrival are ordered forward, consisting of two guns, four companies European Bengal Fusiliers, and a squadron 9th Lancers, to try and cut off a strong mustering of sepoys, who have two guns with them, and who have carried off the treasure from Rohtuck, and are now moving on Hansi. 'Tis said they are 2,000 strong. H. M.'s 75th and 60th N. I. arrived this morning."

Carriage was procured with incredible difficulty, in consequence of the dismissal of the Umballa establishment. Cholera, the Moloch of the East, now broke out, and society was shocked to learn that one of the first victims was the Commander-in-Chief himself. The native mind is given to fatalism, and many were the omens drawn, but not fated to be realized. Since then the amiable and gallant Sir H. Barnard succumbed, and was buried on the crest of the ridge; his feet before the doomed city, which it was not his fate to conquer. The European soldiery, however, were too eager to be at Delhi to sink under the scourge.

The state of the countries around began to exhibit a gloomy change of aspect. Everywhere the veneer of European civilization was peeling off. Crime began to become rife. "Budmashes" swarmed at

Thanesur. The disorganization at Mozuffernuggur and Saharunpore was contagious. District after district in the N. W. Provinces broke up, and, excepting in Saharunpore, where Mr. Robert Spankie martialized law on his own authority, and vindicated the British name by his Avitabile-like determination, scarcely a semblance of authority was left. Bands of ruffians ruled the country. It may be imagined, therefore, that the position of the Divisional Commissioner of the Cis-Sutlej States must have been critical, and one demanding all his talents and energy. Nobly was he seconded by his district authorities. Through them he had to provide the whole of the carriage for the army, and for the siege train from Philour. He had to keep the peace in five large and complicated districts, interspersed with petty chieftaincies, while bands of mutineers were roaming abroad, spreading treason, proclaiming the downfall of British supremacy, and the sovereignty of the army of Hindoostan.

To such a pitch was audacity carried, that a sepoy of the 5th N. I. had the insolence to tear down at Roopur, whither he and others had been despatched ostensibly to keep the peace, a Government proclamation, and urged on the Hindoo citizens the necessity of interdicting the slaughter of kine. A citizen, who lent his support to these views, was at once hanged. In short, there was highway robbery and mutiny at Thanesur; open mutiny at Ferozepoor; outrageous disloyalty at Umballa; panic at Simla. Loodianah was more north; but probably the disreputable inhabitants of this ill-famed and troublesome city had felt the first stroke of the iron rod with which Mr. G. Ricketts quelled disturbances in his district, and won for himself well-deserved reputation. Indeed soon after, so great was the terror of his name, that some inhabitants petitioned the King of Delhi to have him "disposed of," otherwise their lives were not of an hour's value.

In all this extremity of confusion it was casually ascertained that while the Europeans had only ten rounds of ammunition per man, the faithful sepoys were abundantly furnished with sixty! Of the two companies of the 5th despatched to Roopur, to be kept out of harm's way, half melted away on their march. Some, it is said, having well weighed the subject, made up their minds to decamp; and with a proper solicitude for their chattels, had despatched them to various villages; but thinking better of it, albeit some had actually started, they had the effrontery to ask for their property to be re-collected for them by the civil authorities, who were solicited to do so, but declined. This regiment, on the day of the Meerut mutiny of the 10th of May, violently broke open their bells-of-arms, and remained under arms for a whole day; but were pacified, interceded for, and forgiven. The Umballa N. I. corps had also added perjury to their crimes, having actually been re-sworn on their colours. Had they been disarmed or destroyed, much less annoyance would have been occasioned.

To revert to matters previous to the start of the army. Daily telegraph messages continued to prove the vigour of the measures adopted in the Punjab. One came from Peshawur to the effect that a Council of War, consisting of General Reed, Brigadier-General Cotton, Brigadier Neville Chamberlain, Colonel Herbert Edwardes, and Colonel (the late deeply-lamented) Nicholson, all names of repute, had been formed.

A moveable column to quell mutiny at all points was organized at Jhelum, consisting of H. M.'s 27th Foot, from Nowshera; H. M.'s 24th, from Rawul Pindee; an European troop of H. A., from Peshawur; one Light Field Battery, from Jhelum; the Guide Corps, from Murdan; 16th Irregular Cavalry, from Rawul Pindee; and 1st Punjab Infantry, from Bunnoo; Kumaon Battalion, from

Rawul Pindee; wing of the 2nd Punjab Cavalry, from Kohat; half company of Sappers, from Attock.

Events crowded so thickly that its composition was vastly changed, and the above is only given to show how immediate were the preparations. The atmosphere of war had been fully breathed on the frontier year by year; and to be in marching order was an every-day business. For instance, the 27th, H. M.'s, were soon re-called; for their presence was urgent at Peshawur. H. M.'s 24th has since been in constant march and service, but was detained at first at Rawul Pindee. The European troop of H. A. has done service all the way down, and is now within Delhi. The Guide Corps and the Kumaon Battalion both succoured the band of heroes before Delhi. The 1st Punjab, "Coke's," went to Delhi; perhaps fortunately, Coke had been a little disabled before he got there, or else, from his determined gallantry, we could hardly have hoped to count this fine commandant amongst the living. Rothney's 4th Sikhs almost emulated the Guides in the rapidity of their march. Green's Punjab Infantry since went to Delhi. The 4th (Wilde's) was also there by the storm. The march of the Guide Corps* was one of the most rapid on record; some thirty miles a day from Murdan to Delhi, and the force charged up to its walls in the

* For the constitution of this famous corps, vide Appendix.

battle. Alas! that the gallant and well-loved young Quintin Battye, who, too early stricken, died on the field of battle murmuring in the ear of a friend—" Well, old fellow, 'tis the old saying, '*dulce et decorum est pro patria mori*' "—alas! that such youth and promise had not lived to win the ever fresh renown reaped in each fresh contest by his heroic corps.

Gratifying intelligence had been received on the 17th of May of the quiet extrusion of the 4th N. I. from the important hill fortress of Kangra by Younghusband's " Sheredil." None knew of it beforehand. The sepoys looked what they felt, but said nothing. Subsequently they expressed themselves satisfied, on an explanation by Major Lake, the Commissioner; and recently they have distinguished themselves at Noorpoor, when the order for disarming came out, and when no coercion could be employed, by collecting the arms, and conveying them, of their own accord, to the house of Major Wilkie, a mile from the fort. Thus early were all the great military positions rapidly secured one after the other.

Also on the same date the accompanying bulletin was issued:—" Orders have been received from the Chief Commissioner to add 400 men to 18 Punjab and Police Corps—recruiting has commenced. Recruits are pouring into Lahore. The country throughout the Punjab perfectly peaceable and tranquil." It was now manifest who was ruler in Israel. In a totally opposite direction, at Jhelum, the 39th N. I. (since disarmed) were removed from dangerous propinquity to the 14th N. I. (since mutinied, but of whom more anon), and marched quietly to the Siberia of the Poorbeah; the, to him, cheerless unsocial regions of the Derajat. They were amused into the idea that they were going on service. Further mention of this will appear in a future chapter.

Internal precautionary measures having thus far advanced satisfactorily, the telegraph of the Chief Commissioner, himself well cognizant of Delhi, next "urges the Commander-in-Chief to unite the Umballa and Meerut forces, and advance on Delhi, stating *east of the Sutlej we can hold our own.*" In another telegram from Sir J. Lawrence, in answer to a message from the Commander-in-Chief as to what course to pursue, the Chief Commissioner (who was at whist) replied shortly, "*When in doubt, win the trick. Clubs are trumps, not spades.*" General Anson had entertained the project of fortifying his camp at Umballa. At the same time the Commander-in-Chief penned a most elaborate minute for the late Lieutenant-Governor, Mr. Colvin, specifying exactly, from his own intimate knowledge of the notabilities of the Imperial city, who were loyally disposed and who not, with various valuable suggestions. In reply, Sir John received a cold telegraphic message to the effect that "Mr. Colvin had made his arrangements, and that Mr. Greathed, the Commissioner with the army, was apprised of them." "De mortuis nil nisi bonum."

On the 1st of June the annexed proclamation was not without effect as a stay; and it might have rung in the ears of many with prophetic solemnity, for the day of the sepoy army has gone by never to return. The true colours under which they fought have now long since been shown; they were simply armed tools of a Mahomedan insurrection. More than a generation may pass before their folly, as much as their infamy, can be fairly appreciated by their posterity.

From the Chief Commissioner of the Punjab to the Hindoostanee Soldiers of the Bengal Army.

Dated 1*st June*, 1857.

Sepoys,—You will have heard that many sepoys and sowars of the Bengal Army have proved faithless to their salt at Meerut, at Delhi, and at Ferozepore. Many at the latter place have been already punished. An army has assembled, and is now close to Delhi, prepared to punish the mutineers and insurgents who have collected there.

Sepoys, I warn and advise you to prove faithful to your salt, faithful to the Government who have given your forefathers and you service for the last hundred years. Faithful to that Government who, both in cantonments and in the field, has been careful of your welfare and interests; and who, in your old age, has given you the means of living comfortably in your homes. Those who have studied history know well that no army has ever been more kindly treated than that of India.

Those regiments which now remain faithful will receive the rewards due to their constancy. Those soldiers who fall away now will lose their service for ever. It will be too late to lament hereafter, when the time has passed by;—now is the opportunity of proving your loyalty and good faith. The British Government will never want for native soldiers. In a month it might raise 50,000 soldiers in the Punjab alone. If the "Poorbea" sepoy neglects the present day, it will never return. There is ample force in the Punjab to crush all mutineers. The chiefs and people are loyal and obedient, and the latter only long to take your place in the army. All will unite to crush you. Moreover, the sepoy can have no conception of the power of England. *Already from every quarter English soldiers are pouring into India.*

You know well enough that the British Government have never interfered with your religion. Those who tell you the contrary say it for their own base purposes. The Hindoo temple and the Mahomedan mosque have both been respected by the English Government. It was but the other day that the Jumma Mosque at Lahore, which had cost lakhs of rupees, and which the Sikhs had converted into a magazine, was restored to the Mahomedans.

Sepoys,—My advice is that you obey your officers. Seize all those among yourselves who endeavour to mislead you. Let not a few bad men be the cause of your disgrace. If you have the will, you can easily do this; and Government will consider it a test of your fidelity. Prove by your conduct that the loyalty of the sepoy of Hindustan has not degenerated from that of his ancestors.

(Signed)

JOHN LAWRENCE, *Chief Commissioner.*

In the passage here italicised, the wish was father to the thought. Ten thousand overland, then, was worth one hundred thousand round the Cape.

Thus mutiny in embryo was being stifled at almost every station. Perhaps the disarming, par excellence, was that conducted under Major Crawford Chamberlain at the important post of Mooltan. There was no imposing European force present ; there was possibly not sixty available European soldiers. The brigade, of which Chamberlain had to assume the command over the heads of senior officers, consisted of an European company of artillery under Lieut. Smallpage; a troop of native Horse Artillery, under Lieut. DeBude; the 6th N. I., under Captain Denniss; the 69th N. I., under Colonel Hicks; the 1st Irregular Cavalry, under Captain Hickey; the 1st Punjab Irregular Cavalry, under Captain Hughes; and Punjab Infantry, under Captain Greene.

Various sources of information combined in proving that the lives of the European residents were not safer here than elsewhere, so long as the native infantry regiments remained armed. The defences of the fort were not in good repair; and circumstances of the highest suspicion had been elicited.

Sir John Lawrence directed that Major Crawford Chamberlain should take command, and perform that most delicate operation of disarming. The arrangements were perfect, and the highest credit is due to

Major Crawford Chamberlain and his coadjutor, Captain Tronson, of the Katar Mookee Police. Let the critical importance of Mooltan be remembered, containing munitions of war to the amount of 15 lakhs of rupees, commanding the river communication with Bombay, from whence alone reinforcements could arrive to replace the vast exodus of troops from the Punjab, and its position of the last importance, as a check on the Bahawulpoor Chieftain, will be evident. No European aid, even if to be spared, could possibly come 206 miles all the way from Lahore. The Scinde Government was crippled for want of steamers in consequence of the Persian war. The Bombay troops were at Sukkur, 500 miles away.

Here, then, when the first shock of the mutiny was felt, and its extent and character at once comprehended by those in command, eleven-twelfths of the garrison of Mooltan were of Hindoostanee origin! In fact, one European Company of Artillery was at first sight the whole counterpoise to two full regiments N. I., the 62nd and the 69th, the 1st Irregular Cavalry, and the 4th Troop, 3rd Brigade of Horse Artillery. Here, as elsewhere, the cartridge question had been freely canvassed. The Post Office was thronged in an unusual manner every morning by inquisitive sepoys, soon after the disbanding of the

34th N. I. at Barrackpore, which shows a keen anticipation of impending events. Gold mohurs, which can be easily carried in purses of fine cord, were at a premium among them, and family remittances began to be diverted from the usual Government channel to private money-dealers.

These manifestations did not escape the watchful eyes of Major Hamilton, the Commissioner, and Major Crawford Chamberlain. The confidence of the latter in his fine regiment, the 1st Irregulars, was confirmed by information received from a native officer of rank, that the infantry were trying to tamper with his men. The 69th N. I. were most suspected, the 62nd were less so. As to the native troop of artillery (in which favourite service, even before Delhi, few could be drawn from their allegiance), there was every hope of their proving staunch. Captain Spencer, however, did not allow the golden moments of sepoy hesitation to glide by profitless, but set to work, improved the defences of the fort, mounted several pieces of ordnance, organized a battery of two field pieces, and quietly stored provisions for six month's consumption, which had been collected with the utmost despatch by Majors Voyle Hamilton.

The ferries were now more carefully guarded, and

the native correspondence more strictly scrutinized. The contents of one letter led to the execution of the addressee. Suspicious parties were arrested, and the officers in command of the frontier posts of Derah Ghazee Khan and Asnee warned to be in readiness. Captain Hughes, commanding at the latter, seeing the imminent posture of affairs, on his own responsibility at once set out for Mooltan.

By the 9th of June there arrived the 1st Regiment Punjab Cavalry, and a wing of the 2nd Regiment. The disaffection of the 69th, at least, was increasing in intensity, and admitted not the shadow of a doubt. The hour for the disarming was ripe, and on the 10th of June the orders came from the Chief Commissioner; who, as above narrated, exercising his usual sagacious discrimination of character, had selected Chamberlain for the delicate and critical operation. The night was occupied in anxious and secret consultation as to the plan. At morning dawn, the Colonel of the 69th was apprised of the momentous step to be taken, and was directed to parade all the troops in garrison. The admirable operations which ensued, and which called forth the eulogium of Government, cannot be better described than by an eye-witness.

The parade being organized, "The Punjab Cavalry and Infantry marched to cantonments by two separate roads. The cavalry on the road to the right, debouching on to the grand parade, so as to cut off fugitives should the troops about to be disarmed have dispersed before the whole force had assembled; whilst the infantry moved direct on to the parade from the city, and remained concealed until it made its appearance from the rear of the irregular cavalry lines. The troops arrived at their destination most opportunely, and took up their position at the proper moment in the order shown in the annexed plan. (See p. 53.)

"The Horse Artillery were masked by a position of the 1st Punjab Cavalry, and supported by the European company of artillery, the Punjab infantry being on the left flank. The 62nd Regiment N. I., in quarter-distance column, originally occupied the ground to the left of the 1st Irregular Cavalry, but were advanced to the front, the Punjab cavalry taking their place. At the same time, the 69th Regiment Native Infantry, also in quarter-distance column, were marched from their own parade to the grand parade, and halted in contiguous close columns, with the 62nd in front of the masked battery. The whole of these movements were executed without the slightest confusion or hesitation."

So much for the military details, which seem to

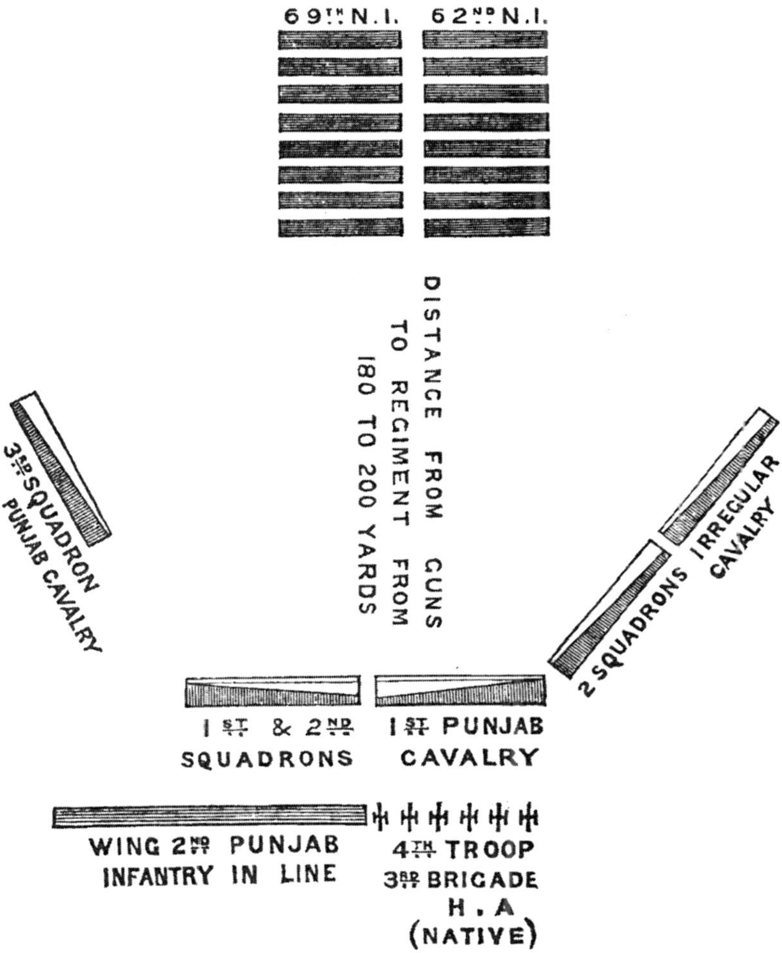
69TH N.I.
62ND N.I.
DISTANCE FROM GUNS TO REGIMENT FROM 180 TO 200 YARDS
3RD SQUADRON PUNJAB CAVALRY
2 SQUADRONS IRREGULAR CAVALRY
1ST & 2ND SQUADRONS
1ST PUNJAB CAVALRY
WING 2ND PUNJAB INFANTRY IN LINE
4TH TROOP 3RD BRIGADE H. A (NATIVE)

defy criticism. After perusal of a general order to the native infantry, Chamberlain rode forward and demanded immediate surrender of their arms, under penalty of consequences. As these words were pronounced, by preconcerted signal, the 1st Punjab Cavalry, by a flank movement to the left, unmasked the Horse Artillery, and six field pieces, loaded with grape, their port-fires lighted, were seen. Each piece, though manned by natives, was supported by eight sturdy Europeans with loaded fuzils. The 62nd piled arms at once. The 69th wavered; the guns menaced; they yielded. The day was won. The disarming of detached bodies, search of the bells-of-arms, and other supplementary acts followed in ordinary course.

The same success attended Captain Tronson, who, with a party of mounted police and some Kuttar Mookhi Police, disarmed a strong party of the 69th at the Treasury.

The self-reliance of the English officer and soldier was never exhibited on a more critical or more bloodless occasion. Though satisfactory, it is nothing to the point, that it was discovered afterwards that the native artillery had without orders laid their pieces with unerring precision full upon the devoted regiments. With such a preponderance of uncertain materials as he had to work with, and such a mere handful of Europeans, this operation managed with consummate tact and resolution by Chamberlain and his gallant coadjutors, stands unique among similar events in the crisis. The inhabitants, who had left the city, at once took heart and returned; their buried treasures were exhumed, and their ordinary occupation recommenced; deputations of the principal inhabitants waited on the Commissioner to express their gratification at the renewal of security and peace.

The general political management of the Mooltan Division, with its varied hosts of warlike clans and tribes, was secure in the grasp of Major Hamilton; and the apparent willingness shown by the chieftains to furnish levies and horses, testify at all events to his own influence, and the general respect for the British power which his administration inspired. In the wild district of Googaira, nothing, up to the date to which this work extends, had occurred. With infinite coolness and determination, at the commencement of the outbreak Lieutenant Elphinstone had promptly disarmed the company of the 49th N. I., who acted as treasury guard, by the aid of the ordinary disciplined police. Subsequently, in July, a daring attempt at outbreak in the Googaira gaol was as sternly suppressed by the same officer.

Strange enough also, since the fall of Delhi, a fierce insurrection broke out in this district, almost as it were in the hour of victory and success, and as if to tax the mental and physical resources of the Chief Commissioner to the utmost. Even this has been extensively, though not without some hard work, quelled and crushed, and the country once more resumed its attitude of sustained activity in preparation for the armies of England, and of stern vigilance against the faintest indicative movement in the chequered drama of Punjab politics.

CHAPTER III.

THE FRONTIER—DOINGS THERE.

VERY early in the crisis, Rajah Sahib Dyal, an old and faithful adherent of the Government, asked the writer how matters looked at Peshawur? The reply was satisfactory. "Otherwise ——" said the questionist, and he took up the skirt of his muslin robe, and rolled it significantly up. The mines, however, had been carefully laid. All that was wanting in the infernal machine, was success in the simultaneous explosion. A rise at Peshawur, and the arrival of some fourteen thousand fanatics, with pillage and murder in their van, was counted upon luckily "without the host." At Lahore, the cry has always been Peshawur is up, and *vice versâ.* With men like Nicholson, and Cotton, and Edwardes on the frontier, small dread could be entertained. Difficulties, however, are apt to be under-estimated, or forgotten, where the victories are those of talents and influence, and the peace and security around are derived from the maturest precautions having been taken against disturbance. For eight hundred miles, thirty or more savage intractable tribes cluster among the wilds and hilly fastnesses from north to south along the frontier. In the hands of Nicholson and Edwardes their political management was safe. Separate interests, separate dialects, and often separate habits and customs, formed elements of political capital, which they were well versed in moulding and wielding. Had the capabilities of these tribes for combination been at all equal to the results which might have accrued from a simultaneous demonstration of one hundred thousand armed and fighting men arrayed, the valley could never have been held. But so stern a retribution had ever been visited on the priest-ridden fanatics by Chamberlain and Cotton, Coke and Nicholson, that they were completely overawed. Moreover, amalgamation between Hindoo sepoys, who formed the majority, with the tribes was (as it turned out to be) full as impossible as the mingling of oil and vinegar. The cartridge question was nothing to the Hill Mussulman. Notwithstanding these favourable dispositions, a critical conjuncture was approaching, and the first note of what had been passing was sounded at the capital, Lahore, as follows:—

"The 55th N. I. have been attacked at Hote Murdan (about 40 miles from Peshawur), officers all safe. One hundred of the men remained true; artillery and cavalry gone in pursuit of the rest, who went away with their colours. Lieut. Law, 10th Irregulars, wounded in the neck. Colonel Spottiswoode committed suicide."

It appears that the first symptoms of disaffection in the valley were exhibited by the 55th N. I. at the bridge guard at Attock; and a portion of the regiment, together with two troops of the 10th Irregular Cavalry, were sent over to Murdan to replace the Guide Corps, which had already marched to Delhi. The reasons for this move are sufficiently clear by the light of recent events. They were utterly in the dark as to the real object; so much so, that when crossing the bridge of boats at Nowshera, they gave vent to their delight in loud cries. Whether this was mere affectation or not, it is impossible to say, but the next morning the regiment taunted the Colonel with having brought them to the fort, as a prison. Colonel Spottiswoode, whose belief in the loyalty of his corps was dearer than life itself, assured them to the contrary, and promised to forward to General Anson any petition they might draw up. The petition was drawn up, and by far the most prominent of all the grievances was the breaking up in practice, though not in name, of the Invalid Establishment. The recent abolition of the European establishment gave colour to the supposition that the native one would meet the same fate.

Meanwhile, the bridge guard under a subadar came into Nowshera in a mutinous state, having refused to obey the orders of Lieutenant Lind, and even threatened to shoot him. It is worthy of record that this very subadar, by name Soodeen Doobey, was a cousin of the subadar-major of the 3rd Light Cavalry, at Meerut, the first appointed generalissimo of the rebel army of Delhi. The cousin had doubtless been selected as prime mover and leader of the hoped-for insurrection in the Peshawur valley. His fate was worthy of his deserts. After heading the mutiny of his corps, he fled to the great Valley, and so wretched an existence did he drag on, that he was fain to give himself up to Major Becher, Deputy-Commissioner of Huzara, with abject supplications for mercy. He was blown away from a gun forthwith.

Major Verner, with a portion of the 10th Irregular Cavalry, went out to meet the bridge-guard, and after disarming, brought them into cantonments. He found the depot of the 55th "skirmishing" all over the place and firing. They had broken into the magazine, and had their havresacks full of ammunition. He ordered his men to charge, instead of which they adopted a retrograde movement. Matters remained thus until the next day, when the remainder of the 55th went off to Murdan, and joined the rest of the regiment there. A sullen disrespectful manner had been detected among the sepoys previously, and reported. The 22nd of May was the day fixed upon for the general rise. In preparation for which, they had sent their wives and children out of the lines.

A suspicious circumstance also had occurred in the 64th N. I., a regiment that had before shown an insubordinate spirit in reference to pay; and the officer commanding the artillery put a picket over his guns, which lay contiguous to it. This regiment, the worst dispositioned of all, on the requisition of Colonel Nicholson (then Deputy Commissioner), was deported (ostensibly) to reinforce the frontier posts of Peshawur. They were marched out, divided into detachments, and stationed under the guns of the three forts held by the Khelat-i-Ghilzies at Michnee, Abozaie, and Shubkudr. Twenty-five lakhs of rupees were in the Treasury, and Nicholson quietly, on the 18th of May, removed them to the fort. This sum, originally destined as a subsidy for Dost

Mohammed, had most opportunely arrived; otherwise, in the financial paralysis which succeeded, it would have been impossible to pay the commissariat expenses.

On the 20th, a letter was intercepted from the 51st at Peshawur (since entirely destroyed), inviting the 64th to come in. The 24th and 27th had had a midnight meeting. Nicholson, bravest of the brave, "bold, resolute, determined," then strenuously urged General Cotton to disarm. The 27th was Nicholson's own corps. The General was not at first convinced of the expediency, until Col. Edwardes arrived at Peshawur from Calcutta, and added his voice to the counsel. Once decided upon, the disarming was carried out with masterly address.

The force was divided into two brigades, each comprising one European regiment, one battery of artillery, and half the troops to be disarmed. The want of English cavalry was so much felt, that Major Barr's troop of Horse Artillery had to be employed as dragoons. At four o'clock in the morning, orders were sent to commanding officers of the native regiments to be disarmed, to hold a parade each on his ground, and while ordinary parade was being held, the Europeans and artillery of each brigade marched down. The order was given, "Pile arms," and they were at once taken possession of and carried off by the Europeans. Colonel Nicholson had opportunely called in the chiefs of the valley, and as the disarming was being carried on, clouds of Affghan horsemen darkened the horizon. So also the peach-gardens around swarmed with armed men, Peshawurrees and hill-tribes, all eager to take either side as the issue might be. The environs of the station, from the cantonment to the city, were literally black with the raffish multitude, on the alert for pillage and murder on the first untoward sign.

They were disappointed; though the cause of the disappointment manifestly increased their respect for the British Government. The measure at once relieved a large proportion of the Europeans, who could now without danger be detached to meet the mutinous 55th and the 64th N. I., supposed to be in mutiny. To leave disaffected regiments armed behind at Peshawur was out of the question. On intelligence, therefore, of the state of the 55th N. I., Colonel Chute, of the 70th, marched thither on the day after the disarming. On arrival, perceiving an armed party forming outside, as if intending to attack, he formed into position; when the adjutant of the 55th N. I. rode up and informed him that it consisted of the loyal remnants of the regiment, accompanied by their officers, about one hundred and twenty in all. The peril of the officers had been imminent. In the night a conclave had been held, and a very small majority had decided in favour of not murdering their officers, who were totally in the power of the sepoys. The remainder of the corps had broken tumultuously and fled towards Soundkhour.

Colonel Nicholson, accompanied by a troop of Horse Artillery, the 18th Irregular Cavalry, one hundred Punjab Infantry, and forty of his personal escort, dashed to the pursuit, slaughtered one hundred and twenty mutineers, captured one hundred and fifty, with the colours, and upwards of two hundred stand of arms. The zemindars behaved wonderfully, and brought in fugitives with their money all safe, and with their heads on their shoulders also, to the embarrassment of the authorities. The sustaining spirit of the chase, Nicholson, was in the saddle twenty hours, having gone over some seventy miles. The mutineers fought desperately when at bay, so that the numbers killed represent the upshot of so many hand-to-hand combats. The terror of his name spread throughout the valley, and gave additional emphasis to the moral effect of the disarming policy.

The conduct of the Punjab Infantry, the 5th (Vaughan's), on this their first trial, was keenly watched. It had a large admixture of the Poorbeah element. It passed the ordeal triumphantly. Shaping their course after the cue thus given by the 5th P. I., the whole Punjab Irregular Force stood committed to deadly hostilities with the Hindoostanee soldiery. The 5th P. I. had the honour of slaying the first mutineer in the black year of 1857. They had the opportunity from local position, and they used it; and their brilliant example set aside all question as to the unsullied fealty of this valuable arm.

After the pursuit of the 55th N. I., Colonel Chute's column moved up to Fort Abozaie, in the hills surrounding which some of the 55th N. I. had found temporary asylum. Here, almost simultaneously with a similar operation conducted by Captain Bingham at the forts of Shubkudr and Michnee successively, Colonel Chute dispossessed the party of the 64th N. I. of their arms. Nothing could have been easier than for the 64th N. I. to have murdered their officers, and to have given up Fort Michnee to the hill-tribes; and considerable discomposure in Peshawur politics would have been the result of such a catastrophe.

The Mooltanee Horse now began to pour in. It has been observed that the 10th Irregular Cavalry behaved disgracefully. Their punishment was adapted to the character of their proceedings. Half the regiment were ordered to Peshawur; the other half remained at Nowshera. The trap was of so masterly a device that escape was impossible. Five hundred fiery and true Mooltanee Horse had left Peshawur for Delhi; while a detachment of H. M.'s 27th were coming back to Peshawur from Rawul Pindee. Each had its cue. They met, and at early dawn fell on the wing of the 10th Regiment, and despoiled them of everything: horse, accoutrements, ammunition, weapons, all but the clothes on their backs! The wing at Peshawur were similarly flayed of all external evidences of the profession they had disgraced. They were then marched down to the Kabul river, eight miles from Peshawur, put into boats, and started off to Attock, where they met their disconsolate brethren. Four rupees a piece were administered, and under escort of the fearless Mooltanees, who required no "orders" what to do in case of attempt to escape, they were deported.

In a previous chapter we have depicted the position of 300 of H. M.'s 81st and 12 Europeans, H. E. I. C. S. guns, as they disarmed four regiments N. I. at Meean Meer. The annexed diagram will show another imposing spectacle. The first terrible evidence of the British Government "*asserting itself*" to the death, was about to be given. A Subadar

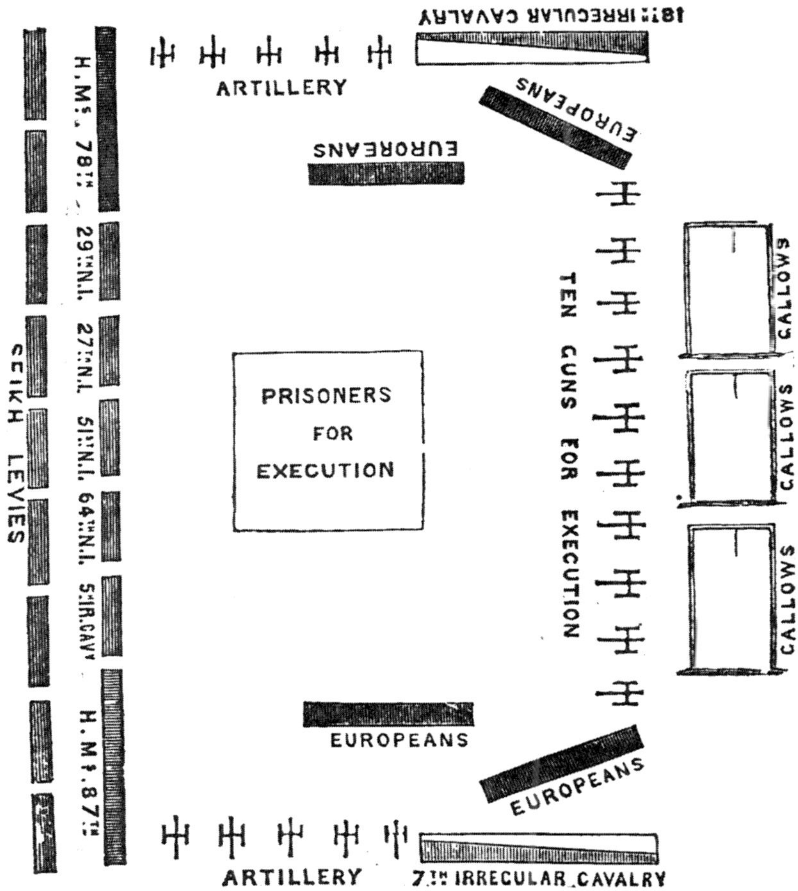
18TH IRREGULAR CAVALRY
ARTILLERY
EUROPEANS
EUROPEANS
H.M'S. 78TH
29TH N.I.
27TH N.I.
5TH N.I.
64TH N.I.
5TH IR. CAVY
H.M'S. 87TH
SEIKH LEVIES
PRISONERS FOR EXECUTION
TEN GUNS FOR EXECUTION
GALLOWS
GALLOWS
GALLOWS
EUROPEANS
EUROPEANS
ARTILLERY
7TH IRREGULAR CAVALRY

Major of the 51st had been captured and hanged, boasting that he had been a rebel for more than a year, and that the English rule was at an end. On this man's person was found 900 rupees. He inquired what was to be done with his money; having, no doubt, in his mind some testamentary disposition to make, and revolving therein the question as to residuary legatees. He was informed that after deducting 84 rupees, the price of the gallows on which he was to swing, the balance would be credited to the State. Twelve men of his regiment were hanged two days after him in a row, on full parade of all troops; and subsequently the awful punishment of blowing away from guns was inflicted upon forty of the 55th mutineers. The pacific English mind will observe the position of the gallows, (See p. 67,) and will comprehend the feelings of the forty doomed men; the last batch of whom had to be dragged up almost senseless to their merited fate. The impossibility of a rescue would, owing to this snug disposition, appear at a glance to the most interested spectators. A Mr. Rich, M.P., moved for a return of mutineers blown away from guns, but the motion was not seconded. General Cotton, who knows no squeamishness, will no doubt be happy to supply him with every information as to the draconic code in force, and which he was the first to execute.

The moral effect of the disarming, on the 21st, was instantaneous and marked. On the 20th of May, Nicholson had despaired of raising recruits; on the 22nd, he was overwhelmed with applicants. As in Lahore, so in Peshawur, the one act formed the political pivot. The people of the country at once decided on their course of policy. The fierce but pliable Asiatic always yields before determined will. Decision pierces him as he shifts. The best-intentioned resident of the Peshawur valley might naturally play the waiting game, in the neighbourhood of an armed Hindoostanee force consisting of a regiment of Light Cavalry, three of Irregular Cavalry, and seven of Infantry. In fact, the mullicks or chiefs of the valley when first summoned by Colonel Nicholson, declined to peril the lives of their followers and furnish aid in the face of such a force. They openly said, "Show us that you are the stronger, and there shall be no lack of support." Within three hours after the disarming-time, to their word, the chiefs of the valley crowded in upon General Cotton, flung their swords on the ground at his feet, and tendered the services of themselves and their vassals.

A suspicious-looking faqueer was arrested about

this time, and a letter, hidden in a small bag, from some one in cantonments to some one outside, was found on him. The contents were that "*this was a time of opportunity; not to fear, but to come in on the day of Eed, for the work was easy.*" He was hanged. Similarly no misplaced leniency was extended to any captures. The offence was mutiny, or the design treason, and, in either, the punishment, death.

The Hindoostanee, formerly sentinel of the Afreedie populace, was now watched by them. The tables, as if by magic, were completely turned. Various threatened confederacies among the tribes were prudently dissipated. A part of the 55th N. I. had been received by the inhabitants of the Swat country; but the Swatees, tired of their new acquaintances, and gradually, for the sake of the reward, the latter have almost all been delivered over and executed. One Subadar, it was narrated, after passing through the process of circumcision, could only fetch four annas two pice as a slave in the hills. Considerable pains had been taken by one of the unscrupulous hillmen to salve his conscience by making a true Mussulman of a Hindoo sepoy he had captured, previous to handing him over to condign punishment before a British tribunal; and he expressed the highest indignation when the convert, in reply to the question of the Brigade-Major, gave his old Hindoo name instead of the new flaming Mahomedan cognomen he had been newly endowed with. The mountaineer shook his fist, and denounced loudly the shocking ingratitude of the apostate, after the disinterested trouble he had taken to secure the salvation of his soul.

It will be remembered that the tenets and practice of the Sikh faith were sedulously framed so as to shock the prejudices of the frontier Mahomedans; and to insure perpetual antagonism between them. This antagonism, even in the same corps of Punjab regiments, has been counted upon, discounted upon, and as yet has always been found solvent. All the Sikhs and Punjabees were taken out of the disarmed regiments, and re-enrolled into a new regiment. Capt. Wilde, on his own responsibility, at once eliminated from his corps the Poorbeahs; an example afterwards imitated in the other Punjabee corps. A regiment of Putthans was also raised. Ten men out of every European company were at once instructed in gun-drill, and the Peshawur Light Horse sprang into existence, mounted on horses from the 5th Light Cavalry, and the disbanded 10th Irregulars.

Intercepted letters revealed nothing by which the loyalty of the 21st N. I. and the Khelat-i-Ghilzies could be impeached, and they were honourably occupied in manning the three frontier forts of Abozaie, Michnee, and Shubkudr. The 21st N. I. subsequently joined in all expeditions into Euzof-zaie. The Khelat-i-Ghilzies filled posts of no mean honour. The moral preponderance of the well-affected in the regiment trampled out the few seeds of disaffection which had been flung among them. This preponderance was not impulsive and momentary, but had all along been deliberate as it was now sustained. No interruption in the usual remittances to their homes in the N. W. Provinces took place. When the mutinous 55th N. I. broke away near the fort of Abozaie, the Khelat-i-Ghilzies were most active in hunting them up. Even the last test was not wanting to prove, beyond a shadow of a question, the discipline and loyalty of the corps. A wretch, named Pahar Singh, seized his musket, and called out that the Europeans were marching to disarm them. The commanding officer and his adjutant made for the magazine, but they were held back by their faithful men. The order was given to load, and unhesitatingly obeyed. A jemadar shouted to the villain to lay down his arms, but in reply was shot dead by him. The murderer was almost instantly despatched by one of the regiment. The assembly was sounded;

not a desertion had occurred: all expressed abhorrence of Pahar Singh's crime. Subsequently, also, when some forty of the remnant of the 51st mutinied and sought protection under a fanatic Syud of Khyber, a body of the hillmen assembled and came down to the attack, but was immediately repulsed.

The total destruction of the 51st N. I. at Peshawur, which occurred in August, will be mentioned hereafter; so that in some measure a sort of chronological order in the narration of events may be preserved.

Certain great causes have doubtless operated in keeping the Swatees, the Peshawurees, and the Kabulees well affected. The assessment of the valley is of lightness to them formerly unknown. The Dooranees ground the people to dust: they do so at Kabul to this day. The Sikhs levied annually twelve lakhs from the valley, and as much more in plunder. The British Government contents itself, and makes the people content, by taking six lakhs per annum, and spending as much monthly! Never, therefore, were the people so prosperous. The ownership of land is eagerly sought for. During the Sikh and Dooranee dynasties every one shrunk from the risk: each tried to prove he was not a landowner. Now every rood is contested. Deeds and bonds of fifty years back are hunted up and eagerly produced. Old claimants from Bokhara and Kabul descend, and try to revive their possessions in the valley. The large expenditure, and the vast number of troops, have opened out a market for cereal produce, as well as for wood and the fruits of the hills: so much so, that the greatest punishment to a fractious tribe is to shut them out from the Peshawur and cantonment markets. It is called "blockading:" every member of the tribe seized in the valley is put into gaol, and 10 rs. awarded to the informer or apprehender.

Another indirect cause of the calm pervading the dreaded frontier may be traced in the fact that at the outset of the crisis the Afreedies had betaken themselves to their mountain fastnesses and cool retreats to escape the hot months. Before they could have been fully alive to the thorough disaffection of the native troops, the regiments had been disarmed and coerced, and Mooltanee horsemen, to whom they have neither liking nor affinity, were coming in daily, together with troops from Bunnoo and the lower portion of the frontier. The astonished Afreedie, instead of receiving his usual intimation of a disturbance, and the when, and the how, and the where he was to take his share, was met by entreaties from relations already snugly enlisted in British employ, to come and take service; for there "were lots of rewards, regular payments, a month's pay in advance, little to do, and that little in accordance with their instincts and prospects of plunder."

The policy of Colonel Nicholson cannot be too much admired. Wild spirits of the valley had become our "right well-beloved and trusty friends." That very populace, in entire and cordial co-operation with which lay the only chance of successful mutiny to the Hindoostanee sepoy, furnished sentinels over them, but too anxious to exhibit their devotion. Richard the Second putting himself at the head of the insurgents, is the only parallel we can call to mind.

Thus all waverers felt that the "Feringhees" had "asserted" themselves. The dâk was intercepted, and then ignorance was as good as a reserve of ten thousand Europeans. They saw Government were utterly fearless and independent of the sepoy army. Many an Afreedie, who had been fighting for us at Delhi, remits the unaccustomed "family remittances" to be realized through friendly agency, and the coin is conveyed to some wild fastness, where an European's life would not be worth a rush. The stimulus of individual prudence acted no doubt quite as well as love for us, and urged adherence to our rule.

Avarice and bigotry are the ruling principles of the Affghan. The former, however, fortunately predominates—the union of the two produces not fusion, but a neutralization of force. They have also an instinctive horror of regular warfare and disciplined enemies. Added to these, the more northern Mahomedans are not so soft and susceptible as the Hindoostanees; and hence their superior intelligence and sagacity rendered them impervious to the idle stories, absurd rumours, and diligent calumnies, which have befooled, excited, and maddened the latter. Moreover, there is no want of generous impulse and lofty chivalrous honour in the Affghan.

As a type of the general feeling which prevailed on hearing of the frantic defilement and execrable outrages on the helpless women, one Affghan, during an interview at Peshawur, spat upon the ground, shut his ears in deep disgust, and congratulated himself that he belonged to a country which had once been the asylum of British captives, but which knew how to treat female honour with courtesy and respect. This unlooked-for sympathy was not confined to mere expressions, but extended to fervent wishes that the British rule might not thus be extinguished amid insult and degradation, but that it might survive to avenge.

Specifically speaking, perhaps, Dost Mohammed is as averse, from motives of sound policy, to meddle with us as Runjeet Singh formerly, or Runbeer Singh now. He had been also receiving a golden subsidy, in the shape of a lakh per month, for the Kandahar Mission ostensibly; and it has not been discontinued. Thus, notwithstanding the entreaties and protestations of his villanous and treacherous family, and Sultan Mahomed his elder brother, "that now is the time to take the Peshawur valley," the old Dost has kept quiet, when one sign from him to the hill tribes would have engendered inconceivable complications; and the people of Affghanistan have acquiesced in his quietude, probably for the reasons above mentioned, possibly because they have not yet forgotten Pollock's avenging army. In Swat a faqueer resides of saintly repute. He, too, is wise in his generation. When Sultan Mahomed played treacherously with Colonel George Lawrence, the Swat faqueer rejected his solicitation to stir up a religious crusade against "infidels." He replied, that, without doubt, infidels they were, but better rulers for the people of the country than the Dooranees either had been or would be. In pursuance of these views of policy, the faqueer allowed but short respite to the 55th N. I. in the domain within his influence, but "moved them on."

Few and far between, at this period even, were instances of bad feeling among the inhabitants. In Eusufzaie the village of Narinjaie has always been troublesome, and its position is difficult of access. There the revenue had seldom been collected without coercion, or show of coercion. They refused to pay the educational cess, on the plea that they did not require education! Then they paid a modicum, and held out for the remainder. Some stragglers of the 55th, and a few "Ghazees," worked them up to open rebellion. A detachment, commanded by Major Vaughan, started from Murdan with the 5th Punjaub Infantry, the 4th Punjab Rifles (Wylde's), 2nd Punjab Cavalry (Browne's), and four guns of the Peshawur No. 7, under Captain Polman. They attacked the village at daybreak, which was desperately defended. After four hours' hard fighting, the whole of the lower villages were taken and burnt. After inflicting this severe lesson, the column retired

A second expedition soon followed, and another castigation was administered. Thus, even with impending convulsion in Hindoostan, and possibly the lower Punjab, the vigour of the frontier policy knew no abatement, but, if possible, was more stern and inexorable than ever. Even the tribes concerned in the melancholy assassination of Lieutenant Hand have knuckled down: they have been heavily mulcted, and have tendered submission. Lately a rebellious "Syud," with some fugitive sepoys of the 55th and 51st, ran the gauntlet down the frontier of each successive tribe, trying to incite insurrection; but they were "passed on!"

The care of the Hindoostanee troops at Peshawur gives the least cause of anxiety, for they are in a cage. There is a fortress on the Rawul Pindee side of the ferry of the Indus, and no one can cross without permission. The disaffected know well that they are hedged in, and if they move they must fight it out to their inevitable destruction.

CHAPTER IV.

JULLUNDUR.

FAR different from the vigour, skill, and promptitude displayed first at Lahore, and afterwards at Peshawur and Mooltan, was the character of the proceedings in the Jullunder Doab. Since the outbreak at Meerut, the 36th N. I., the 61st N. I., and the 6th Light Cavalry, had showed open disaffection; incendiary fires were of almost nightly occurrence. Every device had been tried by the sepoy to try the temper of those in authority, and the result fully justified the conclusion to which they had come, viz., that they could act almost with impunity. It had been whispered that they intended to break out, if Delhi did not fall within a month from the Meerut insurrection. To such a pitch had the disloyalty arisen, that seditious notices, threatening certain native officers who were well disposed towards Government, had one day been found posted up at the Pay Office Treasury, where the guards were relieved daily. The officers alluded to had been specially commended the day before by General Johnstone on parade!

Notwithstanding the urgent advice of the Government that they should be disarmed, the advice was not taken. Infatuated intercessions of the commanding officers were listened to, on behalf of the treacherous regiments. A short period before the mutiny, which will be described in this chapter, a 6th Cavalry trooper had taunted a comrade and the non-commissioned officer with being Christians. At the earnest solicitation of the native officers, who expressed themselves "anxious to maintain the credit of their corps," it was conceded that the man should be tried by a regimental court-martial. He was so, and acquitted! The trooper since signalized himself by firing on his own commanding officer.

On the night of the 4th, the hospital of the 61st N. I. was burnt to the ground. Still, measures for disarming were not adopted, notwithstanding the presence of her Majesty's 8th.

On the night of the 7th of June, a fire broke out in the lines of the 36th N. I. The officer of the day, on going to the spot, found his men loading their muskets, and was shot at by way of reply to his remonstrances. Fires had been of late such ordinary occurrences, that use had become second nature, and some officers did not apprehend any disturbance. A sharp rattling of musketry soon undeceived them. All the Christian population fled for safety to the rear of the guns, which Major Olpherts had judiciously disposed so as to command every avenue; but, on asking permission of Brigadier Johnstone to fire on some mutineers who were coming from the direction of the 36th N. I. lines, he was refused. No want of gallantry was shown by the officers of the regiments in risking their lives in the vain attempt to quell open mutiny by persuasion; and, alas! there was no want of melancholy sacrifices.

The cavalry sowars were the chief instigators of the rebellion here, as at Meerut. They galloped in frantically amongst the men of the 61st N.I., firing pistols in all directions, sounding the double, and yelling that the Europeans and artillery were upon them. The Major, with Lieutenants Tyndall and Kemp, were mobbed; but a faithful few stood by them, and managed to convey them to the quarter-guard, round which a perfect sea of heads was waving. Wonderful was the escape of these officers. Others also were saved through the devotion and presence of mind of a havildar, who feigned severe sickness from rheumatism, and abused the mutineers for disturbing him; Major Innis and others being concealed close by him.

If found, they would inevitably have been murdered. The night did not pass without atrocities. Ensign Durnford has since died from a wound received from a trooper. While the sepoys were busy pillaging the treasure-chest, the havildar alluded to and a drill naick seized the above officers and conveyed them aloft to the top of the quarter-guard, through a trap-door which they shut and sat upon.

Three times had Major Innis, by sheer force of command, stemmed the tide that was rushing to the bells-of-arms. Bungalows were seen in flames in various directions; and a dust-storm added to the uproar and confusion. The Sergeant-Major and his wife had previously got on to the roof of the same quarter-guard. Ever and anon mutineers were heard beneath inquiring for Major Innis, and all the while the unhappy Durnford lay on a charpoy, wounded, concealed by a sheet.

While these occurrences were taking place at the right wing, Captain Basden, with Lieutenant Hawkins, was less fortunate at the left wing. The former was attacked by the sowars, cut at by one, thrust in the arm by another, struck at by a sepoy with his musket, and assailed by a coolie with a bamboo. He rode away only when resistance was hopeless. Lieutenant Hawkins proved himself no mean champion; for, on a sepoy hurling a ghurra at him, this officer charged him, and cut him over the head and neck with a sharp sword. Bethinking him of his revolver, Hawkins went for it, and again came down to the post of danger. He found his regiment drawn up in close columns of companies surrounded by sowars, and when he got within thirty yards, a sentry took aim. Swinging himself low down to the right of his horse, and having the satisfaction of hearing the ball of his assailant pass over his right shoulder, Lieutenant Hawkins administered the contents of a barrel of Colt, and experienced a second satisfaction in seeing his enemy drop. He then rode off to the lines of H. M.'s 8th, charged by troopers and fired at; one bullet grazing his back.

Similar scenes were being enacted in the 36th lines. Young Lieutenant Bates was treacherously shot in the arm, in reply to his vain efforts to appease and control the men. A mournful fate awaited poor Lieutenant Bagshaw, the adjutant, who, while apparently (as he said before he died) almost successful in restoring order, was mortally wounded by a 6th Cavalry trooper. They basely fired on their commanding officer, Major Faddy; previously informing him that "they didn't want him any more."

Similar also was the scene in the Cavalry, and

vain the efforts of the late gallant Willock, the Adjutant, to allay the excitement. Major Mac Mullen was shot in the hand. The general impression at the time was, that the arrival of a troop of Horse Artillery the previous morning from Hosheiarpore had caused a panic, which was fostered by the designing. Reviewing the matter now by the light of subsequent events, there can be no question that it was as base, as deliberate, and as preconcerted mutiny as any which has disgraced the Bengal army; without a single black feature—whether treachery, pillage, incendiarism, or assassination—wanting.

And while the ladies, women, children, and all non-combatants, with the terrors of what had passed in Delhi and Meerut at their hearts, were wild with fear, and the wounded Adjutant Bagshaw was brought in to confirm their worst apprehensions, where was the Brigadier? And what were H. M.'s gallant 8th about, who had been long bursting to avenge their slaughtered countrymen and women? The following facts will serve to point a moral, if they do not adorn the tale:—

It has been previously mentioned that to Major Olpherts' earnest entreaty, to be allowed to open fire upon the miscreants a refusal was sent: a refusal which the native troop did not choose to understand; for on some sowars coming within what they deemed undesirable propinquity, they discharged two rounds of grape with success, but without orders.

All night H. M.'s 8th were kept straining on the leash "on the defensive." Plans of attacks and operations preconcerted for emergencies like the present had been laid down, but nothing could elicit the order for them to be carried out. The fate of all around was uncertain, and yet no movement was made. It was even reported to the head military authority that the guns on the left flank had been actually drawn out, with the express object of advancing against the 36th Regiment, so as to unite with a detachment of H. M.'s 8th Regiment on its coming round, and approval was solicited, without avail. The impression seemed to be entertained by the Brigadier that the outbreak was being adequately quelled by the loyal members of the corps! and orders were issued to act solely "on the defensive." The 6th Cavalry, under the disguise of orderlies, actually crowded in upon the guns, and the lives of the Brigadier and others were threatened; but still, no offensive movement. The mutineers, unmolested, had full leisure (in the vicinity of artillery, and of a Queen's regiment) to squabble about the distribution of the booty, before taking their departure. Such solicitude for the welfare of the gallant 8th, who were eager to be at work, appeared to govern the counsels, that it was with the utmost difficulty Lieutenant Sankey, of the artillery, could, some two hours after the rise, get tardy sanction to reconnoitre with two guns. When they did so, they found the mutineers gone! Grape might have been poured into them. At half-past five o'clock nobody knew what was going to be done. At half-past seven o'clock leisurely chase was given to the fugitives, and Phugwara, a distance of nine or ten miles, was reached by 11 A.M., or twelve hours after the outbreak.

The delay in starting was not occupied in commissariat arrangements probably, as on arrival at the abovementioned spot no rations were forthcoming. The Brigadier observed in regard to the weather that it was hot, and that he should wait until it was cooler. A halt of five and a half hours took place. The mutineers were pushing on fast, and intent on crossing. Exceeding apprehensions were entertained by Captain Farrington, lest the fort of Phillour, an invaluable and strategic point, and containing a large magazine, might have been surprised. But fortunately the fugitives anticipated the keenest pursuit by the dreaded "*gora logue*,"* and contented themselves by inducing the 3rd N. I. to mutiny, which they did, and joined company! The mutineers accomplished twenty-four miles, while their pursuers made seven miles. Instead of standing upon guard idle all night of the 7th, H. M.'s 8th ought to have been started in the cool of the morning at two o'clock. As it was, the pursuing party reached Phillour about nine on the evening of the 8th, and no further advance was attempted until 2 P.M. on the 9th, the next day. All night the European troops were dinnerless, supperless. The whole of the force had not arrived at Loodiana until 11 P.M.

Meanwhile a very opposite line of action had been struck out by the authorities of the Loodianah district; and the contrast only renders the Jullundur operations more conspicuous. Information of the mutiny reached Mr. G. H. Ricketts, C. S., the Deputy Commissioner, by electric telegraph from Umballa: none had reached him from Jullundur itself! He immediately cut down the bridge over the *Sutledge;* and but just in time, for the mutineers had arrived in force on the parade ground at Phillour. The officers of the 3rd N. I. had been warned by some of their mĕn,

* Europeans.

and fled the fort: the regiment, to a man almost, joined the rebels. They seemed to have mutinied as a matter of course and made no attempt to harm their officers. Captain Rothney's regiment, the gallant 4th Sikhs, at once furnished Mr. Ricketts with three companies, to take possession of the Phillour ghâut, under Williams, second in command. Mr. Ricketts also called for two guns from the Nabha Rajah, 100 matchlocks and fifty sowars to guard the ghâut. He then got himself ferried across the river and *walked* from the opposite bank to Phillour; a cool instance of reconnoitring audacity. There he found that the mutineers, baulked by the opportune destruction of the bridge, had left in a body, and had gone to a ferry about four miles higher up. Confident that there must be surely hot pursuit, he recrossed, so as to catch the rebels between two fires, and complete, under these circumstances, their inevitable destruction. Sinister intelligence awaited him. The portion of the 3rd N. I. in the fort of Loodianah and treasury had defied Rothney's Sikhs, had drawn up the bridge of the fort, and levelled their muskets through the cutcherry loopholes. The concerted nature of the whole movement flashed at once on the mind.

Both the fort and city of Loodianah were in

danger. All speedy relief from Jullundur, even under the supposition that any anxiety on the part of the General to close with the fugitives had been manifested, was hopeless, after the destruction of the bridge. The only chance, therefore, was to obstruct the passage at all risks. With this view, Mr. Ricketts and Lieutenant Williams, with the three companies of Sikhs and the two guns, advanced to the attack.

Every moment was of value. It was possible to disperse those who had crossed and prevent their marching compactly on Loodianah, and had General Johnstone moved up, a second Sobraon might have been the issue. One of the Nabha guns was drawn by camels. Twice one of the camels fell, but notwithstanding these obstructions, the brave little party came upon the rebels at about half-past ten at night. They were in a body on the bank among some short jungle grass. Again and again they challenged and met no answer, and finding a body of men steadily advancing on them, they opened a smart fire. Williams arranged his men behind the guns, while Ricketts with his own hands unlimbered one of them. But what with the noise, the flashing of the musketry, and the novelty of their position, the horses got maddened, and either bolted with their riders and limber, or (what is just as probable in those days of treachery) the riders themselves bolted. Still, there was the other gun, a 9-pounder, and Ricketts unlimbered it, and administering a round of grape at the spot where the firing was sharpest, at once dispersed them. Advancing the gun, they blazed away, the mutineers spreading fast, until from a compact body they had thinned out into a large semi-circle. The fight now got sharp, and Williams and eleven of his men were hit. Not relishing too close a contact, all Rickett's matchlockmen and sowars turned tail and fled. The loss of Williams was fatal to further offensive operations, and the ammunition was now expended. There was nothing for it but to retire decently with the gun; which, with incredible labour, and almost entirely alone, was managed. Repeatedly was assistance called for from the Jullundur party, without avail.

Next morning the mutineers advanced on Loodianah, released the prisoners, aroused the Cashmeree population, pillaged the mission premises, burnt the press, and took every horse and pony they could find. But they did not attempt to attack the treasury and the cutcherry; probably having a keen recollection of the previous night's reception. Never was the value of vigorous action more conspicuous than from the single fact that the mutineers, although in the midst of a city favourable to insurrection and uproar and pillage, were so terrified by the attack of Mr. Ricketts, that they dared not measure their strength again, but fled. Had they made a stand at Loodianah and held the fort, their expulsion would have been a most embarrassing task, and the operations before Delhi fatally retarded. But while at Loodianah even, had the Horse Artillery come up, the mutineers could have been annihilated.

As soon as the enemy were gone, Ricketts with a party of horse charged through the city and swept away the rabble; and some twenty Cashmerees, who had joined in the temporary confusion and began to pillage, were summarily hanged. When at last the pursuing force did arrive, the advance was not less languid than before. Everything seemed to go wrong; and with the exception of the check at Loodianah, in which the resolution and conspicuous gallantry of Ricketts and his party probably saved the treasure, fort, and city of Loodianah, all was mismanagement. Three times the mutineers might have been grappled with. At first, in cantonments in Jullundur, when they were permitted to exercise full discretion as to their movements; secondly, at the river, which it took them nearly thirty hours to cross, having only three boats; and again, on leaving Loodianah city.

Thus the energies of fine troops were wasted, the zeal of every subordinate officer was rendered of no avail, the peace of a whole tract of country jeopardized, and the prestige of the British name damaged by —— But we have told the tale.

And so the pursuit ended, and the mortified people of Jullundur returned.

After swaggering, threatening, and trying every experiment to test the metal they had to deal with; unobstructed, except at the river, by the Loodianah authorities, the mutineers marched off in triumph, with colours, arms, ammunition, and plunder, from a cantonment guarded by a European regiment straining to attack them with twelve guns, which opened fire without permission and were stopped thereafter; and by some some six or eight hundred allies belonging to the Kupoorthullah chief. The month that had passed will never be effaced from the memory of the residents of Jullundur. The bare and blackened walls of hospitals and houses of the 61st lines, the silent and deserted streets and over-grown gardens of the once fair station of Jullundur, betrayed evidences enough of audacious disloyalty unchecked; and the disastrous occurrences that rapidly succeeded at other stations, were thereby doubtless accelerated, though they were by no means attended by the unparalleled impunity of Jullundur.

The occurrences we have endeavoured to detail in this chapter excited much newspaper criticism; and it is but fair that the following letter should be republished, in justice to the gallant officer it concerns. High authority, after complimenting in warm terms the gallantry of Ricketts, has pronounced the pursuit a miserable failure:—

TO THE EDITOR OF THE "LAHORE CHRONICLE."

Simlah, July 20th.

SIR,—Illness, consequent on a severe accident which befel me on the 21st of June, prevented my reading or hearing read your papers for more than a month past. Within the last few days I have, however, had the pain to learn that they have contained some severe strictures upon my proceedings, when in pursuit of the Jullundur mutineers.

I will not further notice these at present, than by denouncing them as unjust, and in mentioning that, as a full explanation of my proceedings is before his Excellency the Commander-in-Chief, it would be manifestly improper to enter into further explanation in the public papers regarding them.

I will not, however, deny myself the satisfaction of showing, by reference to circumstances of time and place, that the accusation of delay in my pursuit of the mutineers, and on which accusation probably the whole animadversion rests, is utterly unfounded. The pursuit of the mutineers commenced before seven o'clock of the morning *following* the night of the outbreak. It could not have been undertaken earlier. The direction taken by the rebels was not ascertained till half-past three o'clock. Preparations had to be made in obtaining carriage for the infantry, providing rations, &c., perfecting the equipment for guns, horses, &c., and these, after the utmost despatch of officers, as ready and zealous as men could be, were found impossible to be completed at an early hour.

The complaint of one writer is, I understand, that the haste of departure in pursuit was so great, that the infantry had to march without rations and other comforts, assertions which are true, but which under the emergency are unwarranted, especially as the supply of these deficiencies was left with so able and active a commissary as Captain Sibley. As there was no delay in starting, so there was none that could be avoided in justice to the infantry soldier in the pursuit. From Jullundur to the Sutlej is thirty miles; many of the infantry were on foot, all under an intensely hot sun. By nine o'clock that evening, at the very latest, every man of the mutineers had crossed the Sutlej; by eight o'clock probably the last man had left the right bank.

I ask, is it possible for Europeans to have accomplished thirty miles in thirteen hours (that is, an average of fifty-six miles in twenty-four hours), especially when we consider that they had been under arms the whole of the previous night, and had been much harassed with night duties before that. As it was, they accomplished twenty-six miles in fourteen hours, which appeared to me as much as they were capable of enduring without breaking down. Four miles further would have taken them to the ferry, but I should have had to bivouac them, much broken down, on the banks of a river noted for its unhealthy influences. On the other hand, as much pressed to do (and, I understand, much condemned for not doing), I might have proceeded, but by roads which I have reason to think were almost impracticable for artillery, a distance of nearly six miles to the ghaut where the mutineers had crossed, arriving there not less than five hours after every one of them had crossed, and without the possibility of crossing a single soldier of my own in continuance of my pursuit. Had I, therefore, compassed the whole distance without a halt, a thing utterly impossible, I should only then have arrived in time to see the last boats approaching the opposite bank; but as this contingency involves an impossibility, it need not be dwelt upon. Presuming two hours' rest to have been given to the men, it would be evident from the foregoing that even if their pace under the mid-day sun had been equal to what it was under its mitigated violence, they could not have arrived in time to have overtaken the mutineers, and the result would have left me, after making a false movement, at a great distance from Loodianah. That I halted at Phillour, and prepared for a passage of the river at three the next morning, will not be considered either a delay or a wrong movement. I need not refer to circumstances that delayed the passage, they are explained elsewhere. Suffice it to say that the very appearance of Major Olpherts, with the advance of my force, caused the flight of the mutineers from Loodianah and its neighbourhood, and saved, as I believe, the station from destruction. You will oblige me by inserting this letter in your next publication.

I am, your obedient servant,
M. C. Johnstone, *Brigadier.*

This letter being dated Simlah,* leads me, though not exactly in chronological order, to hark back to the excitement there, and to give a short account of that most indescribable of all circumstances — a panic.

In England the name of Simlah is associated with the notion of a gay mountain retreat, abounding alternately in the charming and majestic, far away from the heat of the plains, and the rumours of disturbances. But it has up to this moment hardly recovered from that grievous social epidemic — a

* While this edition was passing through the press, Lord Panmure, in the House of Lords, adverted to the subject; he stated that Brigadier Johnstone had asked for an inquiry into his conduct, and that the accusations against him had been fully inquired into, and he appealed to the Under Secretary of War for information as to the result. Lord Hardinge replied that the result of the inquiry had been the expression of a strong and decided opinion by Sir Colin Campbell, the Commander-in-Chief, that Brigadier Johnstone had been most fully and honourably acquitted of all the accusations brought against him.

panic. The local journals teemed with acrimonious and recriminatory letters, which we commend to the perusal of those fond of the amenities of literature.

Truth demands the announcement, in justice to much maligned individuals who formed what was facetiously termed the "flying squadron," that there was cause for fear; and the presence of so large a body of non-combatants, not all of equal nerve and heroism, did not tend to diminish it. Harrowed by the recent account of almost simultaneous outbreaks at Meerut and Delhi, their minds were fairly upset by the intelligence that the Nusseree Battalion of Goorkhas, stationed at Jutog, seven miles off, were in open mutiny, and had refused to march when ordered down by the Commander-in-Chief!

Let it be remembered that when his blood is up, the Goorkha is a savage demon; that it is written of this race when the havoc of a Goorkha invasion swept like a hurricane over the hilly regions of the Kangra valley "blades of long grass sprang up, and tigresses whelped in the streets of Nadown;" let it be remembered that the regiment was distinctly disaffected on the cartridge question, and the anxiety of the residents to learn how negociations were being carried on at Jutog may be justified. Now, they heard that an advance of pay had been peremptorily demanded, and as submissively accorded; now, that they had coerced their officers, whose lives were despaired of, and had gone so far as to mob the Commanding Officer; now, that the doctor had taken command; again, that seeing they were masters of the situation, they were inventing the most trivial and preposterous pretexts against marching, pretending that the removal of their guard from the Government Treasury indicated (as it certainly did) a want of confidence, and that the loan of some of their arms for the defence of Simlah signified (and unmistakeably) that it was themselves that were feared and against themselves they were to be used.

"About twelve armed European soldiery and civilians," wrote a correspondent to the *Lahore Chronicle*, "were collected to defend the Bank and the helpless ladies and children of Simlah, of whom not less than one hundred were congregated before nightfall. The scene of distress and confusion that ensued is almost beyond description." "The church bell was rung, signal guns were fired, and scouts were galloping to and from Jutog all night. Three different times did the mutineers commence their march on Simlah, but a merciful God restrained them."

Subsequent to this, on the residents learning that one of the terms acceded to by the contracting parties was, that the arms lent to them should be returned, and the Government Treasury replaced under their charge—all heart and presence of mind were lost, the panic reached its climax, and general and precipitate flight commenced. Officers in high employ rushed into ladies' houses shouting, "Fly for your lives: the Goorkhas are upon us." Simlah was in a state of consternation: shoals of half-crazed fugitives, timid ladies, hopeless invalids, sickly children, hardly able to totter, whole families burst forth, and poured helter-skelter down on Dughshai and Kussowlie. Some ran down steep khuds and places marked only by the footprints of the mountain herds, and remained all night.

The mental hallucination of one gentleman, who possessed a telescope, was remarkable, since he actually saw the Simlah bank on fire, and depicted to his agonized auditors, after the manner of Rebecca in "Ivanhoe," the Goorkhas charging up the hill. Another returned from Subathoo and informed Captain Blackall that there had been heavy firing at Simlah, and he had seen the smoke of several houses burning.

Never had those stately pines looked down upon, or those sullen glens and mossy retreats echoed with such a tumult and hubbub. Ladies who are now placidly pursuing ordinary domestic duties, wrote off "perhaps for the last time" to their distracted husbands in the plains; then, snatching up their little ones fled away, "anywhere" out of the Simlah "world." Extraordinary feats were performed: some walked thirty miles! Some, alas, died from the effects of exhaustion and fear.

A bhistee, suffering also from an optical illusion, declared that he had seen the first European murdered in the bazaar. But it is perfectly true that one gentleman, an officer, met a drunken Goorkha who drew his "kookree" (a weapon as crooked and ugly as its name), upon him in the bazaar. The effects of the panic are not yet obliterated in the minds of domestic servants; who, fortified by the doubtful aspect of affairs in the plains, soon acquired the most insolent demeanour. Anecdotes became rife and significant of what was passing in their minds. One little boy was told that his mamma would soon be grinding gram for the King of Delhi!

It may be remembered as an instance of the prevalent impression among Mahomedan domestic servants particularly, as to the inevitable and complete overthrow of the English, that the khansamah of General Hewitt, who had been in his service for twenty years, the instant the outbreak commenced, started confusion on his own account by flinging all the plates from the dining-room into the air, dancing with joy, and pocketing the silver; when the aide-de-camp, Captain Hogg, entering the room at the unusual uproar, suddenly allayed his transports for ever by killing him on the spot!

This, however, is a digression, and we must return to Simlah and the Goorkhas. Four months have elapsed since the above turmoil, and this very regiment having done effective service in the plains, it is due to those interested in the welfare of the corps to exhibit one or two features in the case by the light of their present good conduct. There are extenuating circumstances, and now-a-days one cannot afford to be chary of trifles: the telescope must be knowingly put up to the blind eye upon occasions, and the behaviour of all Goorkhas has been but slightly if anything inferior to Europeans.

The present, then, was the first instance in which the Goorkhas had been ordered down *en masse* to service in the plains: a company had always been left to protect their families during their absence. Constitutionally jealous and sensitive, as all hill tribes, to the honour of their wives (notwithstanding the palpable security derived in the peculiarly ill-favoured physiognomies of these gentlewomen), the Goorkhas hesitated. The proceedings of the residents, distinctly pointing out the former custodians of the place as the present enemies to be feared, was aggravating enough. A chest of arms, so it is said, had been clandestinely deported from Jutog, and powder also had been as furtively abstracted at Simlah. Picquets had been posted; and an advanced picquet stationed at Boilleaugunge with videttes up to Jutog. Guns were pointed also up the Jutog road. A mistrusted man is inclined, if in power, to pay people off for their want of confidence. The Goorkhas, no more than "Lady Teazle," affected to relish suspicion without a cause. General Penny had actually assumed command on the night previous to the exodus. The Simlah Bank was fortified, and was all but impregnable, with stout hearts and steady rifles, even against two regiments.

But General Penny's command was soon at an end. Conciliating policy prevailed. The Goorkhas, as an evidence of full confidence, demanded that they should be put in guard over and in the bank, in which lay some 80,000 Co.'s rupees. The critical and uncertain aspect of affairs may be imagined not only from the audacity of their demands, but the undisguised audacity of their bearing. They demanded to be shown the actual treasure, and their swarthy features lit up with glee unpleasant to the eye of the bystander, when they saw the shining pieces. One sepoy tossed back the flap of the coat of a gentleman present, and made a queer remark on the revolver he saw worn underneath.*

The late Commander-in-Chief now took the matter in hand. The time for coercing and disbanding regiments he thought had gone by. The Goorkha Corps had always been a great stand-by to the Government; and in a crisis like this some stretch might be allowed to retain men who had no more affinities with the Poorbeah than the European—perhaps less. The

* "The Goorkhas," wrote an excellent authority, "helped themselves to 16,000 rs. from the Government Treasury, which was afterwards conceded to them on the pretext that it was an advance. They took possession, or had possession given to them, of the Government Treasury, and for some time would not let a rupee out of it." At Kussowlie, the Hill station just above Umballa, affairs were equally, if not more critical. The Deputy-Commissioner of Simlah inquired of the Assistant-Commissioner of Kussowlie (Mr. Taylor), whether it would not be better to move, with all European officers, soldiers, &c., to Simlah. To this policy, as likely to create unnecessary alarm, Mr. Taylor was strenuously opposed; deprecated the ignoble effect it would produce. Simlah being forty miles off, Kussowlie became the especial prey to distressing rumours as to the behaviour of the Nusseeree Battalion. The commanding officer at Dugshai wrote "emergently" to Captain Blackall, H. M.'s 75th, for troops. Three officers passed through Kussowlie armed to the teeth, and scared the public

Jutog men were on the point, if not in the act, of open mutiny, and their examples might be fatal to the Kumaon and Sirmoor Battalions and the 66th, from which good service was expected, and has been obtained. In this strait the Commander-in-Chief selected Captain Briggs, the Superintendent of Hill Roads, who possessed an intimate knowledge of the habits, customs, and feelings of the inhabitants, and much influence therefrom, to act as mediator and plenipotentiary.

He was empowered to hold communication with the Goorkhas, to endeavour to conciliate, and assure them that any expressed grievance or apprehension would be redressed and allayed; to appeal to their characters as soldiers, and to do "anything" to

by stories of their having nearly to fight their way down. The Goorkhas at Kussowlie were in open mutiny, and there might have been bloodshed, if Mr. Taylor had not stopped Captain Blackall from ordering in a party of H. M.'s 75th, reminding him that the safety of the residents of Simlah depended on not a drop of blood being shed. Captain Blackall acknowledged the wisdom and judgment of the advice, and contented himself with being prepared for the defensive. The safety of the inhabitants of the station was admirably cared for at Kussowlie by this officer; who kept his temper, and acted with great presence of mind, though surrounded and taunted by the Goorkhas with such expressions as "Shot for shot!" "Life for life!" Almost directly, in short, to the address and temper in parley of Captain Blackall, and to the wise counsel of Mr. Taylor, do the residents owe their escape from horrors, in which, in enormities perhaps, Cawnpore would have been outdone.

suppress their excitement. He had thus full confidence placed in him. This officer must have had to encounter enormous difficulties, and a state of feeling bordering on frenzy; and it is fortunate that the end justified the means so amply in the present instance for the retention of any regiment of any sort at the price of wholesale condonation of mutiny.

The concessions extorted involved a sacrifice of the dignity of the Government, which the speciality of the crisis alone can atone for. Even on riding up the hill on his pacific mission, Captain Briggs fell in with the Kussowlie party of Goorkhas. One of them put a musket to his head; on which he talked argumentatively on the ignoble success of slaughtering a single man. Disarmed by his *sangfroid*, the Goorkha solaced himself and Captain Briggs with the remark, that in the morning he and his brethren would do as he hinted, and slaughter every European. To change the subject he asked them for water, which they gave him, and while partaking themselves he rode on ahead.

On mature reflection, Captain Briggs decided that pacification at all risks was necessary; the lives of the officers of the corps, those of the crowds of non-combatants, and even of the whole hill population, he deemed at stake. Suspicion and mistrust he considered had been instilled into them by those adverse to the British power, and fostered all over India by a concurrence of accidental causes; by which probably was meant the want of confidence, not unnatural, shown by the Simlah residents.

Among the most remarkable "concessions" was the dismissal of one Chunderbun, whose offence consisted in having compromised his corps by stating that they had no objection to use the cartridges! Major Bagot was of opinion that Chunderbun was the best soldier in the regiment, and was, moreover, absent from Jutog on the day of the mutiny. He was recommended to mercy as one willing to "serve in any regiment in India, and undoubtedly a first-rate soldier." Suffice it to say, with this exception, a free pardon was given to the regiment generally, and belief in the "loyalty and soldier-like qualities, for which the corps had ever been distinguished," was accorded. The cartridges were then and there destroyed, and the fresh ones hereafter always made up on the parade-ground. Two men "dismissed by order of court-martial, for taunting the school of musketry," were restored to the service. The conduct of the native officers in not bringing to notice the dissatisfaction which existed, was pardoned; but Subadar Chunderbun, who had said his regiment had no objection to the cartridges, was removed, as above mentioned.

In order to show that the end has possibly excused the means, the accompanying quotation of Charles W. Chester, Adjutant, is reprinted, exclaiming "against the malicious falsehood of those who (at Simlah) insulted the regiment by displaying a quixotic amount of courage, and then made off so gallantly, and now seek to justify their want of judgment and pluck by the grossest misrepresentations." Further, on June the 17th, the following extracts will show that the position of Captain Briggs was delicate, and that the remarkable behaviour of the Goorkha, in weather as abhorred by him as by Europeans, only adds to the series of anomalous events which chequer the page of 1857 in India. It is from the *Lahore Chronicle*:—

"Previous to the 15th of May (says Captain Chester), the regiment had never shown the slightest symptom of disaffection. They have never shown it since. The men have marched double marches; from their small numbers, every man in addition has been on daily duty. They have suffered severely from fever and cholera without a murmur. They have captured the men who robbed the Kussowlie Treasury, and expressed their indignation that any one should escape without severe punishment. They have reported the men of the 5th N. I., who instigated them to mutiny, and on their report that regiment was disarmed. And now they are encamped at Saharunpore" (then almost totally disorganised), "the safeguard of the district; relied on by every European; feared by every turbulent native."

Mention has been made of the fort of Phillour and its timely salvation. It was orignally a serai, and is situated on the Grank Trunk Road. Runjeet Singh converted it into a fort in his days; the position commanded the river Sutlej by the addition of a *fausse braie* and ditch all round, and bastions at the four corners of the enceinte. The northern gateway was protected by a continuation of the ditch in front, in a demi-lune form, with a drawbridge. Shortly after the fort was acquired by the British, in 1846 (at the time the Jullundur Doab became ours), it was converted into a magazine of ordnance; chiefly guns, mortars, shot, shell, &c., the powder being stored in the fort of Loodianah on the left bank of the river. When the mutiny broke out there were within its precincts some sixty or eighty heavy guns and mortars of sizes, in addition to several light guns; also immense quantities of shot and shell.

Let it be remembered that the first siege train, a third class one, had to be furnished for the operations against Delhi ; and the complication that would have ensued, but for the almost providential safety of the fort of Phillour, will be conceived. It was garrisoned at this critical conjuncture by a strong guard of the 3rd N. I. Facts subsequently elicited showed that the 3rd N. I. designed to seize the fort at the pre-concerted signal. But the providential precipitation of the affair at Meerut disconcerted all such treacherous designs, defeated some, baulked others, and led to checkmate in detail of all ! The Jullundur troops were to have seized the station of Phillour, and there was nothing to operate against such a position but H. M.'s 8th Regiment.

On the 12th of May, Brigadier Hartly, commanding at Yalund-kai, resolved to occupy the fort. Accordingly at dusk on the date mentioned, he despatched a small detachment of H. M.'s 8th and a couple of H. A. guns off from Jullundur, which reached Phillour just at daybreak, twenty-four miles. The gate was open ! Unconscious grass-cutters quietly going in with their loads were followed in closely by the Europeans and guns. So dumb-foundered were the native guard that they could not collect sufficient presence of mind to turn out and give the ordinary salute. To Major Baynes, commanding the detachment (after Brigadier Hartly), is due the safety of this most important fortress. It is to be hoped the warning of having such strongholds as Lahore, Govindghur, Phillour, Delhi, Allahabad, without overwhelming proportions of European troops, may never have to be repeated. Had Major Baynes not at once comprehended the preciousness of time, and arrived so opportunely and swiftly as he did, there is every chance that the move would have got wind; the troops in the station would have mutinied, rushed into the fort, and murdered every European conductor in it. No time was lost in ordering off the detachment of 3rd N. I.

It is credibly reported that the seizure of the fort had been planned for the very day on which they were ousted by Major Baynes. When the Jullundur mutineers, as previously narrated, reached Phillour on the 9th of June at gun-fire, the officers of the 3rd N. I. were in cantonments, and tried every endeavour to get their men to turn out of their lines, to oppose the advance of the 6th Light Cavalry; but in vain. Lieutenant Tayler, on hearing some reports of the mutiny from the Thannadar, had galloped out about a mile and a half from the station, and returned post-haste to arouse Colonel Buller and his men to the fact. But the men refused to obey any orders, and at last the cavalry advance had actually reached the butts. At this juncture a celebrated athlete and champion in the regiment roared out to the men to advance and welcome their comrades. They did so: a few remained and cautioned the officers to be off, as all was over. Anticipating seemingly a hot pursuit, the mutineers made little attempt to damage the station, and none to attack the fort; nor, with the exception of a few cavalry troopers, did they attempt to cross the river at this point, but marched leisurely higher up: their subsequent movements, the supineness of the pursuing column on the right bank, the gallantry of the attacking party on the left, have been detailed sufficiently.

Phillour Fort having been thus saved, and the Talundhur Doab evacuated, the Commissary of Ordnance, Lieutenant Dobbin, was busy up to the end of August in supplying all sorts of material—heavy guns, enormous supplies of shot and shell, musketry and rifle ammunition, entrenching tools, in addition to every sort of weapon of warfare—to the continued stream of Irregular Horse and Foot, which kept issuing from the Punjab on their route to Delhi. When the gallant Neville Chamberlain (at this period the predecessor of his lamented friend Nicholson, as Brigadier-General commanding the moveable column) reached Phillour, he found the fort in a dilapidated state.

Accordingly, on the 20th of June, Lieutenant Oliphant, of the Engineers, commenced work, and notwithstanding the extreme scarcity of labour, he continued to strengthen all the parapets for guns, opening the embrasures and widening and defending them by massive logs and trunks of trees; and by the latter end of July, besides being amply provisioned, the fort bristled with twenty heavy guns in position, including howitzers; in addition to nine light guns at various angles.

The following is an interesting statement communicated to the compiler by the excellent Governor of the Lawrence Asylum, who was in a most responsible and anxious position in the hills:—

"Early in May we were alarmed and horrified by the news of the atrocities perpetrated at Meerut and Delhi. The natives said, 'It is because of the annexation of Oude, and the Poorbeas will all rise, and then what will become of the Europeans?' They seemed shocked at the horrible atrocities committed, but not taken by surprise by the mutiny. Soon after, news reached us that the Nusseree Battalion at Simlah were in a state of mutiny. The natives said,

'They are good men, and do not wish to rebel; but if the Company's *raj* is over, what are they to do? If they fight for their salt, and it turns out that the mutineers are victorious, what will become of them? Every man must take care of himself.'" There can now be no doubt that it was this feeling which caused the otherwise inexplicable conduct of the little Goorkhas at Simlah; besides which they had a number of Poorbeahs among them, through whom they were continually incited to mutiny. Some of the hill Ranas were in the same state of uncertainty, and apparently waited to see which side the Rajah of Patialah took. This chief took two days to consider before he decided to cast his lot in with the Government. There can be no doubt but that if this chief had proved recusant all would have been lost in the hill stations.

"On Saturday the news was brought in, that the Goorkha guard over the Kussowlie Treasury had looted the treasure and made off. One of our chuprassies, who was bringing up a box of clothing to the institution, met a body of twenty-eight Goorkhas at the village below the Asylum on the Simlah road about one mile distant. They had with them the treasure, and were collecting coolies to carry it on to Simlah. They abused and beat him, and threw down the box, asking for rupees; but on finding no sound was emitted by the concussion, and being assured that there was nothing in the box but clothing, he was allowed to pass. That night at the Asylum all the women and children were collected in the girls' house as being most capable of defence. The male inhabitants of Sunawur and the elder boys were mustered, and spent the night in alternate watches. It was an anxious night, for intelligence was received that 200 Goorkhas were *en route* to Kussowlie to assist the Treasury guard, who had sent off messengers for them. Early on Sunday morning, 17th May, I rode off to Dugshai to arrange for a retreat to that station in case matters became serious. Whilst there conferring with the commanding officer, an officer rode in from Subathoo with the intelligence (which proved groundless) that the massacre at Simlah had commenced, and that the cannon could be heard from Subathoo.

"Orders came for the force at Dugshai and Subathoo, and the inmates of the Asylum, to concentrate in Kussowlie. The officer commanding at Dugshai determined to hold his own; but on the evening of Sunday the 17th we retreated to Kussowlie, where the party was accommodated in a couple of empty barracks. We remained there ten days; till the

Goorkhas, who in the meantime had decided on the side of loyalty, marched down to Kalka, when we returned, with no other damage than some loss of health from having been cooped up in ill-ventilated rooms. The whole period was one of intense anxiety — anxiety which, though somewhat relieved by the departure of the Goorkhas, has been kept up by the constantly arriving intelligence of one sad disaster and horrible catastrophe after another, until the recapture of Delhi has given us fresh assurance and comfort.

"As far as our experience here goes, the native servants have behaved admirably. With one or two exceptions we have very few Mussulmans here, about eight or nine only, and these table servants and bhisties. In my own family I found our table servants more attentive and orderly than usual, although, in common with ourselves, sufferers for the want of money consequent on the plunder of treasuries. The bunniahs, too, and native contractors, never lost their confidence in the power of Government, but always said—'Sahib it is but for a little while, and all these rebels will bite the dust,' (literally eat dirt), 'for the Company is almighty.'"

"Our position was also one of considerable difficulty on the score of supplies. All communication ceased, and the usual supplies of cash with it. The markets were closed to credit, and there was little ready money; and but for the prompt assistance of the Local Government, which cashed in anticipation our drafts on the Supreme Government, we could not have existed much longer, as the contractors had at length parted with their jewels and ornaments to procure supplies. Our losses by the mutiny are severe indeed—10,000 rupees per annum by the lamented death of Sir H. M. Lawrence alone, and about 5,000 per annum more by other mournful casualties.

"The feeling of intense anxiety has now given way to gratitude for God's great mercy to us. With 380 helpless little ones about us what could we have done if attacked at Sunawur? and to what place would rebels, bent on the destruction of the European population, have been so likely to direct their attention in the hope of cutting off at one fell swoop so many? The whole European population of these four stations must have been (at the time of the outbreak and after the greater portion of the troops had marched from thence), less than 250. Only about 100 men were left at Kussowlee, about 50 or 60 at Dugshai, and less at Subathoo! What could such a force have effected, if the hill chiefs had concentrated their forces behind us?

"The Asylum has been kept in a state of siege up to the present time. A little force of police has been organized, with a native superintendent at their head (a Poorbeah, but a faithful man); and the Europeans capable of bearing arms formed a Volunteer Corps, and took alternate rounds four times nightly. This has now been discontinued. I must not omit to mention that we were all obliged to evacuate the station, and to leave our houses with our property behind us. The males and many other natives voluntarily formed a corps for the protection of the property, and so faithfully guarded it day and night that nothing was missing when we returned.

"Some Poorbeah coolies wished to loot, but were told by the leader of this little band, that if they attempted any such thing they would have to kill them, the guard, first.

"Before and during these troubles, faqueers were every where seen about the neighbourhood; and I have since learnt that they were emissaries from Oude and Delhi, empowered to offer seven rupees per man to any willing to enter the service of the respective pretenders to sovereignty. About 100 coolies employed at the Asylum went off to Oude in consequence, and small drafts of Poorbeahs have been continually leaving the hills during the whole period for Oude and Delhi. The hill men around us have proved perfectly quiet; the inhabitants of the large village, from which Sunawur take its name, offered to despatch to our assistance fifteen or twenty men when required, and this is a Brahmin village.

"At the time of the Murree outbreak (a little before that event I think) there were some unpleasant reports respecting an intended outbreak of the Mahomedans, in which the household servants were implicated. Whatever might have been the truth of the report as to the intention, nothing came of it in action. They knew we were all prepared to fight to the last, and all on the *qui vive*, and perhaps thought that 'the better part of valour is discretion.'"

CHAPTER V.

MUTINY AND ENGAGEMENTS AT JHELUM AND SEALKOTE.

Rough hewn as were all human devices in the vast struggle, Divine Providence shaped their ends. Apparent weaknesses were turned into sources of real strength; foolishness became wisdom. The Jullundur evacuation placed H. M.'s 8th and artillery at the disposal of the Government to reinforce the army of Delhi. It would be easy to show how the events which will be described in this chapter, have, though terrible in individualities, tended unmistakeably to the prosperity of the general issue of the great stake at risk. The very vigour of the action of the Government, though it recoiled, or rather eddied in various quarters against itself, ensured ultimate victory. Almost all commanding officers, while confident of the "staunchness" of their own corps, appreciated the luxury of the vicinage of one of her Majesty's regiments; and as often as not acquiesced in the propriety of the disarming any other regiment but their own. The masterly way in which the sepoys had been outwitted at Lahore, and the summary and fierce retribution visited on them at Peshawur, contrasted with the tempting accounts sedulously spread of the exodus scot-free of their *bhai-bunds* at Jullundur. Those regiments in the Peshawur valley felt the thing hopeless: they were in a cage. Not so the 14th at Jhelum, or those at Sealkote.

The first intelligence of the Delhi and Meerut outbreak reached Jhelum on the 13th of May.

The troops at that station were entirely natives, of Poorbeah extraction—Major Knatchbull's native field battery, the 14th Regiment N. I., and the 39th Regiment N. I.

Against such a force, had they chosen their time for mutiny and massacre, resistance was futile, for at Jhelum there is not a building capable of withstanding cannon. A faint hope, however, that the artillery might remain staunch was indulged, so the magazine was fixed upon as a rendezvous; its situation being midway between the civil and military stations. Major Clement Browne, the Deputy-Commissioner, urged from the first the quiet removal of all ladies; but without avail. The worst news was withheld from them mercifully. Of the commanding officers, Major Knatchbull appeared confident of the fidelity of his men; Colonel Gerrard was assured of the good feeling and conduct of the 14th N. I.; Colonel Macdonald, with more reserve, did not think that the 39th N. I. would fire on their officers! The proposition to intercept sepoy letters by the Deputy-Commissioner was not acceded to, for fear of precipitating the danger. Anxiety was the order of the day, and every eye turned to watch the measures of the local Government. Proofs abundant of the vigilant and sagacious minds at the head of affairs were not long forthcoming. And comfort was soon derived from the evidence that the Government not only was prepared by superior genius and force of will to anticipate and baffle, but to quell and punish every indication of mutiny at home, beside sending aid to other parts of the empire. In pursuance of this policy, orders instantly came forth for the 39th N. I. to depart in light marching order to Shahpore, where further orders would await them.

The wondrous agency of the electric telegraph was brought into play. But for "God's lightning," simultaneity had been added to spontaneity, and the empire was not worth a week's purchase. The Delhi revolt was thus known to the authorities long before the swiftest-footed miscreant could herald the tidings of its success. The relief experienced by the European residents in getting rid of the 39th N. I. before it was common talk, may be appreciated, when it was found out that there was every reason to believe that on the receipt of the looked-for signal a conspiracy to murder all the Europeans at night would have been carried out! The 39th were despatched purposely by the most circuitous route on the left bank of the river, so that all communication with the station and the dâk road was cut off. The regiment thought they were selected for service against some petty chieftain. Their progress was anxiously watched. Ahead of them was a mutinously-disposed detachment of the 46th N. I., in charge of the treasury at Shahpore. If the 39th N. I. were allowed to communicate with them, a junction might be effected, the treasure lost, and the example followed; or, which was just as bad, that when required to march across the Jhelum, with the knowledge that they were destined for Dera Ismael Khan, they would refuse payment, and so bring on a mutiny at that remote point. Measures were taken to prevent any mutiny between the men of the two regiments by sending the Shahpore detachment out of the way, and the 39th marched on without the exhibition of any reluctance: moreover, with the exception of a small party of thirty-three men left at Jhelum to protect regimental property, and which were mixed up in the mutiny at that station, they have apparently continued to conduct themselves in an orderly manner; even to the giving up of their arms, when required by Colonel Macdonald.

The march of the 39th Regiment was immediately followed by the arrival of a moveable column composed chiefly of Europeans. Their short stay produced decidedly a good effect; in no way weakened by the removal, under its protection, of the native battery, soon to be disarmed at Lahore. The station was now left with the 14th Regiment; and these men were watched very closely, notwithstanding the opinions loudly expressed by their officers of the fidelity of the regiment. Intelligence was received from various sources, unsuspected by each other, and each excellent. Day by day, the necessity for this espionage became more and more apparent. For a time they remained to all appearance staunch, for there were two parties in the regiment. Then came nightly meetings, at which first one and then the other opinion prevailed in debate;—the turbulent party were ready to seize any pretext for flinging the regiment into mutiny, and at one time nearly succeeded in doing so, because there was some delay in the issue of the pay from the non-receipt of the abstracts. Being made acquainted with the internal politics of the corps, Major Browne was enabled to adjust the difficulty, by informing Colonel Gerrard, and inducing him at once to apply for the pay in anticipation. Other symptoms of ebullition were communicated to the Chief Commissioner, who at length deemed it necessary (though no overt act had been committed), as a precautionary measure, to disarm the regiment.

Accordingly a detachment of 250 men of H. M.'s 24th, under Colonel Ellice, three Horse Artillery guns, under Lieutenant Cooke, and a portion of Irregular Mooltanees, under Captain Lind, were ordered to proceed to Jhelum for the purpose. The well-known 24th had suffered more exposure since the outbreak than perhaps any other corps. If the adage be true that more is done in campaigning by legs than arms, two notable instances of this truth will be found in this chapter. On the commencement of the outbreak, the regiment marched to Wuzeerabad, but, owing to apprehensions at Peshawur, had to return on the 8th of June. Then three companies, under Major Woodhouse, were ordered to Attock, perhaps the hottest place in Upper India, situated on ground upon which no tent can be pitched, and affording only accommodation to the European soldier in the natural excavations which abound; and wherein it is a question whether the stifling heat from radiation is not less endurable than the sun itself. In these ovens the three companies were stewed up for a month; when, in consequence of the departure of the detachment under Colonel Ellice for Jhelum, they were ordered to Rawul Pindee by forced marches. The first night they marched thirty miles; but as no carriage adequate was procurable, no less than twelve soldiers perished from apoplexy and sun-stroke. The detachment under Colonel Ellice was to arrive in the cantonments a little before daybreak to effect the disarming; but unfortunately it arrived when the sun was up, and the 14th had got wind of their fate. No sooner did the head of the European column emerge into sight than the 14th N. I. at once commenced a dastardly firing on their own officers, who fortunately escaped. The late Colonel Gerrard, it is surmised, in full trust of his men, informed them of the object of the European arrivals, and forthwith they fell to loading.

Under such circumstances, it was a thousand pities that the Europeans were not halted for refreshment, and simple picquets placed around to prevent escape. As it was, a most desperate, unusual, and protracted engagement immediately ensued, in which the most determined gallantry was shown on our side. Every inch of way had to be fought, and the mutineers, fully armed, had to be bayoneted (like rabbits from their burrows) out of their huts; from which they were firing with telling effect on the men in the open space, through loopholes obviously of long preparation.

The fire of the six-pounders was making little impression on the buildings to which the mutineers had betaken themselves. The most rapid and determined fire was poured upon the Europeans, with deadly effect, from every nook and corner behind which the enemy skulked. The quarter-guard was the chief stronghold. Round the roof of the building was a loopholed parapet which commanded the whole line.

The European force was out in the open, and Colonel Ellice felt that but small progress would be made, with this position in the enemy's possession. Heading a small and brave band, he charged and took the place with a cheer. But his bravery nearly cost him his life, he being most dangerously wounded; and the loss of the commander at the critical moment created confusion. He received a shot wound in the neck, the ball coming out close to the spine; another through his leg, and his horse had been shot under him. The Mooltan Cavalry also had made a splendid charge; but the business of the day was not one in which cavalry could be effectual in sweeping up streets, when the enemy were lodged in houses. They afforded considerable aid to the Deputy Commissioner, Major Browne. Meanwhile, the elimination of the Sikhs from the 14th N. I. had taken place, and joined with the police under command of Lieutenant Battye and Lieutenant Macdonald, they behaved splendidly.

The harassing work of clearing the lines it was found impossible to effect without considerable loss. Lieutenants Streathfield and Chichester were both wounded, the former pierced through both legs in a gallant attack on a temple. When driven out, the enemy retreated to a walled village, too close to which, as was now seen, the cantonments had been originally erected. Before this village the lamented Captain Spring fell mortally wounded. The out-works of the village were easily taken; but as the mutineers were fighting with halters round their necks, they fought like stags at bay.

Satisfied with the impression made, and aware that there must be a limit to heroic endurance of fatigue —the Europeans having fought desperately for 12 successive hours after a long march of 12 miles, and being 20 hours under arms, 13 of which they were fighting without a morsel of food—Captain Macpherson determined on bivouacking on the bare ground for the night. His anticipations of the impression made were correct. The next morning all had fled. One hundred and fifty dead bodies were counted on the field, and thirty were brought in the day after. Each had died in almost hand-to-hand conflict. The police despatched numbers on islands, and one hundred and sixteen were executed. It is said that some one hundred and odd of the 39th N. I. were fighting with the mutineers. Thus ended a bloody struggle in which the hopelessness of a native sepoy force, although fighting to the death behind walls, contending against determined Europeans, was again evinced. As a fit conclusion to the Jhelum affair, a specimen of the sort of correspondence is afforded, by which it will be understood how the trammels of "red-tape" were at once broken through in the Punjab.

An assistant commissioner captured a party of the mutineers of the 14th, who had fled from Jhelum, and addressed Mr. Robert Montgomery as to their disposal; that high functionary appended on the reverse the laconic order required, signed with his initials only, there being no time for delay: the same order being as laconically endorsed by Sir John Lawrence, G.C.B., Chief Commissioner for the Punjab, also with his signature in initials. That order was for the execution of the extreme penalty of the law :—

"*Jhung*, 11*th July*, 1857.

"MY DEAR MR. MONTGOMERY,—

"We have caught a native officer and nine sepoys of the 14th N. I.; of these one stabbed himself in the boat, and falling or jumping into the river was drowned. Another some time after cut his own throat, leaving one native officer and seven sepoys to be dealt with according to the law.

"I have written to you publicly on the subject, and intend proceeding to try these mutineers immediately on their arrival. Their conviction is beyond a doubt. The only thing is are they to be hanged here or blown away from the guns elsewhere. I shall feel much obliged if you will send me speedy instructions on this subject. In the interim I am scouring the country in every direction, and trust that not one of the murdering scoundrels may escape this way. They were armed with muskets loaded and capped. Fortunately the anxieties they had undergone, and the pangs of hunger, had put it out of their power to do mischief. All is quiet here. I have nothing further to add save that I hope to receive your authority to my punishing these mutinous dogs as they deserve, by return of post.

"Yours sincerely,

"H. L. HAWES."

On the reverse is :—

"I have ordered them all to be hanged —R. M."

"All right.—J. L."

The conduct of Maharajah Goolab Singh on this occasion was not calculated to afford the purest satisfaction: it was thoroughly Asiatic; which will convey sufficient meaning. One hundred and eighty-one mutineers had escaped into his territory, and he guaranteed their lives. After about two months and a half, Goolab Singh died; the turn of the tide then disgorged one hundred and twenty-one: the remainder having been allowed to be at large, by him or his officials. Many acts of doubtful hue and sufficient significancy had been brought to the notice of the Chief Commissioner, even up to the actual plunder of some frontier villages in the Goojerat district. But it was politic to wink at these things at the time: we had not the whip hand of events so perfectly as now.

The people at Jhelum were in feverish uncertainty for some time previous to the outbreak, and afforded opportunity for the exercise of the utmost tact on the part of Major Clement Browne; but their disposition towards our rule was uniformly excellent. The revenue was paid with unusual punctuality; and even when the zemindars heard of the temporary need of Government for ready money, many sturdy village elders came forward and volunteered to pay in anticipation their autumn rents. A posse of headmen of the remote collectorate posts actually formed a guard, and escorted money to the treasury at Rawul Pindee. Crime had not increased; and under this severe test, contentment with the British rule, and the appreciation of peace instead of turbulence and uncertainty, might fairly be assumed as proved in the Jhelum district. One remarkable trait was elicited. All the old rebels of the Sikh war, who were under a sort of official and social ban, seized the opportunity of regaining their characters; and naturally nourishing a hope that their loyalty might evoke substantial recognition, came forward with offers of service. No man hopes to regain confiscated land from a State he thinks tottering to its fall. Many of the most dangerous thus, as it were, drew their own teeth for danger; and were absolutely made of capital use. But to resume the narrative.

Intelligence of the Jhelum affair, as it progressed, was transmitted through the ever faithful telegraph to Nicholson, at Umritsur with the Moveable Column. He considered it his duty at once to disarm the 59th Native Infantry; which was accordingly simply effected under the guns of Govindghur. On the same day, the occurrences at Sealkote, now about to be detailed, broke out.

On the 10th of May, the garrison at Sealkote, one of the largest military stations in the Punjab (bordering on Kashmere), was composed of one troop of Horse Artillery (Colonel Dawes), one light field battery (Captain Bourchier), both manned by Europeans, H. M.'s 52nd Light Infantry (Colonel Campbell), the 9th Light Cavalry, 35th N. I. (formerly of the illustrious garrison), and the 46th Native Infantry.

Brigadier Brind (of Punniar, Moodkee, Ferozshuhur, Sobraon, celebrity, and of Ramnuggur, Chillianwallah, Goojerat, where he held a brigade) was in command. This was one of the stations whither detachments of different sepoys had met, as at Umballah and elsewhere, to practise with the new Enfield rifle. A fair opportunity of learning each others' sentiments of the cartridge was thus conveniently afforded; and so favourable a one for disseminating treason never so fortuitously occurred. On the formation of the Moveable Column, H. M.'s 52nd L. I., the European Artillery, the 35th N. I., since disarmed, and the wing of the Light Cavalry were detached.

Brigadier Brind protested against the European troops being entirely removed, and desired that 250 should remain. In reply he was requested to disarm. But to the last he shared in the belief (almost glorious) in the honour of the sepoy; and again and again has this belief been shaken in the face of dispassionate observers. Setting aside the military objection, that the presence of small detached parties of Europeans without direct communication (when the whole European force in the Punjab amounted to scarcely above 7,000 men, to overawe a population of 14,000,000, and 27 districts), was contrary to all military rule—250 Europeans against a determined number of a full native regiment and a wing of cavalry, could make but little head under any circumstances; and to stand on the defensive anywhere was not the policy in the Punjab. Under these considerations, the smaller risk had to give way to the greater: the loss of a district must be chanced when an empire is at stake. By consummate tact and show of confidence, the lamented Brigadier postponed the dreadful day. Every politic device had been seized and acted on to prove that no mischief or disloyalty, was apprehended. Letters even were forwarded as usual, and not withheld by the postal authorities as in other districts.

It was known at Lahore on the 12th of May (although the majority were well disposed) that a vague fear occupied the minds of sepoys that orders had been issued from "London" to ruin their caste. A proposition, indeed, to massacre a large party assembled at Brigadier Brind's house, had been actually on the tapis, but was postponed until it was shown "whether" they would be forced to bite the obnoxious cartridges. This was the handle that worked (but too precipitately) the leverage of national, or rather Mahomedan, concerted rebellion. A downright Anglo-Saxon apology, that the "composition" was a mistake, was as powerless before the countless insidious influences at work and the grand unsuspected design of dominion at bottom, as the efforts of the mop of Mrs. Partington against the Atlantic Ocean.

Let it be recorded in the history of the late Bengal army that, unappalled by stories of other regiments, unshaken by the atrocities around, the officers of each several regiment stood by their colours; and hundreds have perished from their devotion, hoping where none could believe. Scanty as, by system, were they in numbers; small, as from circumstances necessarily arising from that system, might have been their real influence; never amid the dark recitals of the morning's papers did they quail from their post, or fear for any but the women and the children. Human nature vindicated itself, and rewarded them; for in almost every broken corps there have been instances of fealty and devotion at which the heart can feel even glad.

The precedents at Jullundur and Ferozepore show

that the presence of even a whole regiment of Europeans was not enough to prevent mutiny; though probably their easy vicinity (before the rivers rose, and with the Umballa regiments openly disloyal) to the great seat of disease Delhi, was no small incentive.

At Sealkote the withdrawal of European troops at this peculiar crisis gave our ally, Maharajah Goolab Singh, an assurance of the highest policy in the faith reposed in his loyaly. The trust was, on the whole, not misplaced; for never has greater attention been lavished on the visitors of the valley than during that interval. Before his death he furnished a contingent and money. His isolated position permitted him to keep aloof; and though doubtless conscious of the Mahomedan fanaticism which was the prime mover of the sepoy revolt—nay, more probably, intimately forewarned as to the details of the concocted scheme—this potentate, wisely perhaps for himself, certainly with profit to us, kept outwardly and seemingly, as far as an Asiatic can, his pledges with the British. His conduct to his nephew, Rajah Jawahir Singh, had been only lately stigmatized in terms of strong disapprobation by the Lahore Government; and it is just possible that the presence of that personage, with some 1,500 bayonets in the capital, might have been a source of alarm to Goolab Singh. Anyhow, Goolab Singh was appeased and friendly, while Jawahir Singh has furnished active assistance also.

Up to the date of events at Jhelum everything had been still and quiet as deep waters at Sealkote. The band played as usual; society partook of its evening recreation. In fact the sepoy did not find it worth his while, as at Jullundur, to test by insolence and incendiarism the temper of the authorities; for he was already master of the situation. Society knew, however, the corruption that lay beneath that shining and polite exterior. The sepoy, too, felt himself suspected, and knew his power. Besides this a hopefully hypocritical aspect had to be worn. By a temporising policy, every day without fresh evidence of "overt" disaffection was of a week's political value. And though every resident in the ill-fated station had his or her forebodings, none liked to dilate upon them, when every gesture and look was commented upon. Thus on the night of the rise, the Superintending Surgeon begged a friend with whom he was dining, who had remarked on the contemptuous demeanour of the sepoys, not to let "his fears get the better of his senses." The next morning the slaughtered body of Dr. Graham fell into the arms of his daughter, shot dead by a trooper as he was driving her to the fort!

Whether or not the events at Jhelum, as to the desperate resistance made in the lines of the 14th N. I., against the small force of Europeans, had been communicated to the troops at Sealkote; or whether the matter was of deliberate concert for that day, is a matter of guess. But it is certain that a man connected with the wing of the 9th, forming part of the Moveable Column at Umritsur, who had inprudently obtained leave, was the immediate cause of the insurrection. He brought the stories of the disarming of the 33rd and the 35th N. I. He must have inflamed the passions of the cavalry by every sort of lie; for a second conclave was held with delegates from the 46th N. I. that very night. The whole plan of the morning's bloody proceedings must have been then laid out. The sepoys invited their officers to hold an inspection parade, the invitation was complied with, and the right wing at once commenced firing on them; though, providentially (or let us hope for the sake of human nature, purposely) without effect. As at Meerut and Delhi and Jullundur, the cavalry were the prime instigators; their powers of locomotion alone achieved more than the most elaborate persuasion. They rode to the infantry lines, flashed off their pistols, shouted rebellion, yelled about religion, cursed the "Feringhee kaffirs;" and intentionally committing themselves they committed the best intentioned others.

There was not an European inhabitant in that station that had not his or her plan of escape or defence; though it is deeply to be deplored that no concerted plan for a general house of refuge and defence had been pre-arranged. At early dawn ominous sounds of musketry were heard, and in less time than takes to pen this, each European individual had commended his soul to God, and prepared for the worst. The organization of the mutineers' plan was soon fearfully apparent. Before daylight, skirmishers and cavalry pickets had been posted at all outlets, to prevent the escape of a single victim. There was nothing to be done, for about one hundred miscellaneous Europeans, with women and children, but to flee as best they might to the small fort, which fortunately existed at the station. None hardly who reached that place of refuge had not been fired at; and to the anxious greed of the mutineers to seize and divide the treasure, and to the confusion consequent thereon, may be attributed the safety of so many lives.

But the gallant old Brigadier could not be induced

to retreat with undignified hurry, though in the presence of inevitable death; he was thus easily caught, and shot through the back mortally. Captains Chambers and Balmain were chased, and bullets flew around, past, and beneath them. The kind-hearted Captain Bishop was murdered in sight of refuge underneath the fort; the assassin reloading deliberately after his first shot, to finish him as he was trying to cross the stream, almost in the presence of his agonized wife.

The daughter of the murdered Superintending Surgeon, Miss Graham, owes her life to one of those extraordinary but too scarce incidents of the late crisis, when the personal attendance of some troopers and sepoys had succeeded in saving life. Fortunately having taken refuge in, or rather being dragged shrieking to the cavalry guard, she found there Colonel and Mrs. Lorne Campbell surrounded by a few faithful troopers, who escorted them safely to the fort.

So complete had been the conviction in all minds apparently of the annihilation of the British power—the uncentrical situation of Sealkote, the absence of all healthy current of civilized ideas, and its contiguity to a despotic Government of the worst repute, favouring the impression among the people—that an offer of two thousand Company's rupees a month was made to Colonel Campbell to take command of the mutinous regiment down as far as Phillour! A similar offer had been made, varying in the amount of pecuniary emolument, to Colonel Farquharson, with leave to reside in the hills!

Whilst there was comparative safety for the crowd of miserable fugitives of all classes in the narrow, miserable fort, amid the wounded, the dead, and the dying, but little solace could be acquired in the contemplation from the ramparts of things outside, or hope for the many still absent. All the neighbouring villages, roused by the tales of the restoration of the Mogul dynasty and the extinction of British power, emptied their hordes upon the ill-fated station, and left it a complete wreck. This once splendid cantonment, with its enormous public and private property, first became a scene of deliberate waylaying and cold-blooded murder, and then the theatre of havoc and ruin.

For fourteen hours the families of Dr. Butler and Captain Saunders, with eight little children, crouched in an out-house in their garden while search was being made for them. The whole house was pillaged in their hearing, fired at, and riddled with shot. An old Sikh "chowkedar" saved them from inevitable murder and outrage, by calmly informing the pursuers that they were not at home. Dr. Butler shot a man of savage aspect, who peered through the only grating which admitted light and air into their hiding place: the man fell, groaned, but spoke no more, or all would have been discovered. In those terrible thirteen hours a mother had so disposed herself, her baby in her lap, her three children behind her in a row, that haply one bullet might kill all at once. It appears that a party of the 46th N. I. had concentrated, at the sound of the bugle, for their work. The shocks caused by the explosion of the magazine, added to the smashing open of the venetian blinds, of panes of glass, wardrobes, and furniture, mingled with the rattling of the troop of the cavalry, and the ringing of their sabres and scabbards, (the door of the retreat being occasionally battered at), all caused a chaos of inconceivable uproar and alarm. And this was going on in fifty different places at once. Even a babe in arms had been sent away with its faithful Sikhhee wet-nurse, in the hope that in the almost inevitable massacre that little one might be saved! The good and revered missionary, the Rev. Mr. Hunter, wife and child, were cruelly and foully assassinated; and another surgeon of the same name as the Superintendent, Dr. Graham, was also murdered.

The isolation of Sealkote has been spoken of, and was probably one of the complications and difficulties that beset the civil authorities, in addition to the marked plurality of Hindoostanee *employés*. Elsewhere the Government natives have been trusted, tried, and found true metal; here they had succumbed to the arts of the seducers. Even the loyalty of the Sikhs "quailed." The gaol was broken open and its denizens let loose, and the work of riot and demoralization seemed complete. The new levies in the fort, however, remained true. Emissaries had been despatched to General Nicholson. The state of affairs was critical. Every house was gutted, many were unroofed.

Short, however, was to be the triumph of the rebels, and great the contrast which two days hence the appearance of their remnants half-drowned, naked, and dispersed, was about to present, skulking into the fastnesses of Cashmere. Their cupidity had been their ruin: the "*embarras de richesse*" swamped them. Alarmed by the menacing vicinity of H. M.'s 24th (though but a slender wing), uncertain as to the position of the Moveable Column, and the probability or not of its moving on Sealkote, they abandoned the intention which they had at one time entertained of attacking the fort. This so-called fort was a mere mud work, and could not have stood for an hour against the 12-pounder iron gun, which the mutineers had in their possession. They had counted upon the distance of the dreaded "*gora logue,*" H. M.'s 52nd, at Umritsur; they had counted upon the chance of the 2nd Irregulars at Goordaspore* turning faithless; and upon the hope of easily securing the co-operation of the 4th N. I. at Kangra, and the 16th Irregulars at Hoshiyarpoor. They had also counted on the actual presence in the Moveable Column, of the wing of the 9th Light Cavalry, and on the embarrassing presence of the 59th N. I. still, in their apprehension, armed at Umritsur, and thus affording subject for guarded movement on the part of Nicholson.

Possessed with these confident anticipations, in brief ecstacy, off marched the 46th N. I. and the left wing of the 9th, bugles sounding, banners flying, and laden with stolen property, leisurely towards imperial Delhi. But their Nemesis was on the alert. They had not counted on the forethought, the wisdom, and soldierly genius of the lamented General Nicholson.

On the very day of the outbreak, (the 9th July,) while the 14th N. I. were fighting for their lives at Jhelum, he had a third operation of disarming, and

* Still armed.

the 59th N. I., a distinguished regiment, succumbed to the general fate. Previously, under the shadow of the fort at Phillour, the significant mandate to *pile arms* had been unresistingly obeyed by the 35th and 33rd N. I. So also when the Sealkote mutiny came to the ears of the General, the baffled wing of the 9th Light Cavalry were quietly disarmed; and, perhaps, a hundred and fifty more truculent visages never paraded face to face within one yard of as many open and frank-faced Anglo-Saxon soldiery.

The position of a commander, who has to disarm a regiment and a half of the column under his charge, is not an ordinary one in the annals of military history; and for a commander to march against marauding cavalry, without a branch of this arm in his own force, is next to impossible. This wing of the 9th marched along for nearly six weeks with the Moveable Column, hugging the belief that their wiles were unsuspected; and the promptitude of their treatment at the proper time was a master-piece of checkmating. The policy adopted before that was, perforce, of a temporizing nature. The position of these regiments in the Moveable Column was always so adjusted that H. M.'s 52nd and the artillery could make mincemeat of them at any given signal. So sudden had been the crisis, so wide and far-spread had been the disaffection, that to counteract it at once was a physical impossibility; for the counteracting force had to be created. Thus there were no reliable cavalry even to replace the wing of the 9th just disarmed, and hardly men to mount their horses when the column* marched to the scene of victorious action at the Trimoo ghât.

General Nicholson had adopted a centrical position at Umritsur. Its presence overawed the Manjha, the nursery of the warlike spirits of the Khalsa soldiery; it rendered hopeless any movement of the 59th N. I.; it could afford immediate aid to Lahore and to Goordaspore; and, as will now be seen, it could crush mutiny, and save the whole Doab from anarchy.

The station of Goordaspore is forty-four miles from Umritsur. Determined by a bold stroke to assert the might of British power, General Nicholson formed the project of making for this point in one forced march under a July sun. And nobly did the gallant H. M.'s 52nd and the ever-ready and brave European Artillery, relieved by occasional lifts in ekkas or on horses, perform their toilsome march:

* 3rd Troop, 2nd Brigade, Horse Artillery; three guns No. 17 Light Field Battery; H. M.'s 52nd Light Infantry; detachments 3rd and 4th Punjab Infantry; 1st Company Police Battalion, and two newly-raised ressallahs.

they knew their man. Numbers fell out from exhaustion; apoplexy and sun-stroke did their sure work on others; but the distance was accomplished. On arriving it was found that the mutineers had got as far as a place called Noorkote, about fifteen miles from the station. A trap was at once devised. They were permitted to cross without molestation.

At 9 A.M. intelligence from reconnoitring parties reached head-quarters that they had fallen into the meshes, and were crossing in force at the Trimoo ferry, never known to have been fordable previously at this season of the year. The river Ravee was rapidly swelling, and enhanced the chances of complete discomfiture. The distance to the scene of action, again to be marched, under a tropical sun, was nine miles. The enemy were sighted at midday.

Calculating, doubtless, on the armed wing of the 9th Light Cavalry being with the column, and on the mutiny of the 2nd Irregulars, they had drawn up in a bold and imposing line; their right resting on a serai and a dismantled mud fort; their left on a small village and clump of trees; the cavalry pretty equally distributed in flanks. The British force advanced as follows:—Three guns Light Field Battery in the centre; the troops of Horse Artillery equally divided 100 yards on the sides; and 300 men of H. M.'s 52nd, with Enfield rifles, in extended order at one face between and on the flanks of the Artillery; and the remainder of H. M.'s 52nd, with the Punjab Infantry, with the rear and reserve.

The enemy opened the action by charging down boldly up to the flanks of the guns; obviously expecting their brethren in the rear. The struggle was fierce and brief. A British cheer uprose, the bayonets came into play, and the universal result occurred, whether against French or Russian, or against disciplined recreants from their colours. The rebels turned and fled: one hundred and fifty corpses strewed the ground. The advancing tide proved a faithful ally, and swept away as many in their flight. The Sikhs flew like vultures on the ill-gotten spoil of two days before, which was left on the field.

Mindful of the extraordinary march of the troops, and his want of reliable cavalry, Nicholson wisely decided on awaiting further news of the rebels' movements; Lieutenant Boswell being left to keep watch with his detachment of Punjabees, while Captain Adams and other officers reconnoitred. The former officer had to indite a letter to the General on an important move that he discerned among the enemy: having no ink he wrote in blood, which was fresh and plentiful around him!

However, the complete and sudden downfall of the main body was soon apparent: arms, uniform, accoutrements, had been flung away in dismay. After their first and only conflict with the dreaded "*Gora logue,*" all hopes of martial progress to Delhi were abandoned. Some three or four hundred, hemmed in by the rising flood and maddened by failure, resolved to die at their post on the island. So in the morning Nicholson crossed his force half a mile down the river, keeping the mutineers' gun in play by his artillery higher up. They were attacked by the detachment of H. M.'s 52nd, in skirmishing order, and with a few men wounded the affair was over. The khansamah, (or *chef de cuisine*) of the late Brigadier Brind plied the 12-pounder gun on H. M.'s 52nd, who at once doubled and captured the gun. This was the signal for the promiscuous flight of all who could run away, and the slaughter of all who remained. Thus ended the action against the Sealkote mutineers. The political effect was immediate and decisive. But for the want of cavalry it would have been the most complete stroke of business ever effected.

There was no want of characteristic incidents. Carriages (in one of which was found a bottle of *eau-de-cologne and a Bible,* and an unfinished overland letter) had been appropriated by the new fangled military chieftains; who with fire and sword were about to march unmolested to the imperial city, and aid in supplanting the empire of a century. One desperado of the 9th Cavalry galloped up to an artillery sergeant, saying, "Salaam, Brabazon Sahib," and slashed him over the head, inflicting a wound of which he afterwards died. Another sturdy horse artillery man, suddenly discovering that the sanctity of the rear of his guns was outraged by unlicensed intrusion of the enemy's troopers, swept three in succession of their horses to the earth with his spunging-rod.

Short shrift awaited all captures. The motto of General Nicholson for mutineers was "*a la lanterne.*"

Lieutenant Baillie, of the 55th N. I., and Lieutenant FitzGerald were wounded, but altogether few casualties clouded the bright record of their skilfully-planned and successful achievement.

At Sealkote, Mr. Montgomery again caused to be administered the only panacea to the hydra-headed disease; and foremost among those who suffered various punishments, were the rissaldar of the cavalry, a Sikh, and the subadar of the Sikh Police Battalion, for not doing their duty, and the gaol darogah (a Hindoostanee). The duty of trying these men by commission was no ordinary one; and then the position, the rank, and the country of two of the offenders were taken into consideration. They received previous to sentence a fair and lengthened trial. Had there been the faintest hesitation shown in bringing them to trial because they were Sikhs, or any tendency to relax the construction of the law, the effect would have been most dangerous. But the Judicial Commissioner knew not what it was to swerve from the right line of action; and fearlessly did his delegate, Captain Lawrence, perform the stern duty of presiding over the trial, and of sentencing to death two of his own subordinates. Thus the impregnable stability of the State was acted upon throughout as a given axiom. No overtures have been made that were not in accordance with this line of policy, and in keeping with the tone of international communication with all civilized countries. No concessions have been made.

CHAPTER VI.

MUTINY OF THE 26TH N.I., MURDER OF MAJOR SPENCER, AND TOTAL DESTRUCTION OF THE REGIMENT.

ONE of the most portentous features of the insurrection in Hindoostan, was official ingratitude and disloyalty. We have read of judges and collectors mocked with a trial and murdered deliberately by their native official subordinates, principally, if not always, Mahomedans. Even in the Punjab, as detailed in the last chapter, where the people are as yet on the whole loyal, the execution, by orders of Mr. Montgomery, of a subadar of a Sikh Battalion, of the resaldar of the mounted police, and of the gaol darogah for "*having failed in their duty to the State*" was necessary, to show publicly in the eyes of all men, that at all events, the Punjab authorities adhered to the policy of overawing, by a prompt and stern initiative (the only way to strike terror into its semi-barbarous people), and to the last would brook nothing short of absolute, active, and positive loyalty. Government could not condescend to exist upon the moral sufferance of its subjects.

In contrast with this was the real service rendered, and the official loyalty displayed, by the tehseeldars, police officers, and even common moonshees of all grades, in the Umritsur district.

The effect of the victory at Trimoo had begun to wear off. Up to the end of July, there had been a lull in mutinies and outbreaks in the Punjab. To attempt it, with Nicholson in the vicinity, was felt to be sheer madness. But again the fatal poison was about to break out for the third time, at the lunar interval of one month; and the doom of what was once one of the most disciplined and distinguished of the native corps was about to be sealed.

The 26th N. I., stationed under surveillance at Meean Meer, was, as previously narrated, disarmed on the 13th of May last.

Whether there had been any preconcerted scheme among the disarmed regiments for a general attempt to escape from their unpleasant position, is not known; though it has been generally understood that lots had actually been drawn, and that had the 26th succeeded in any measure, the 16th Grenadiers had engaged to follow in their wake. Some say that the noon-day gun was to be the signal of a general rise. Society, on the 30th of July, was, however, shocked to hear of another foul murder of a commanding officer, Major Spencer, and the rise of the 26th Regiment. Lieutenant Montague White narrowly escaped. He was enticed into the lines by some sepoys, who affected sorrow at the murder, and was about to dismount, when a warning voice in his ear told him to beware. He galloped off; but not before some hand had aimed a felon stroke at him, and wounded his horse. The sergeant-major was also killed, and the regiment precipitately fled; a dust-storm (as was the case at Jullundur when the mutiny arose) raging at the time, favouring their immediate escape, and concealing its exact direction.

They were not, however, unmolested; and it is feared that the ardour of the Sikh levies, in firing when the first outbreak occurred, precipitated the murders and rightened all, good, bad, or indifferently disposed, to flight. From subsequent statements, since taken down, it is concurrently admitted that a fanatic of the name of Prakash Singh, alias Prakash Pandy, rushed out of his hut, brandishing a sword, and bawling out to his comrades to rise and kill the Feringees, selected as his own victim the kind-hearted Major; of whom it is said that he was quite overcome when the order for disarming this corps (which thus furnished his own assassin) was at first communicated to him. Another panic arose at Anarkullee, and the thundering of cannon at Meean Meer into the then empty lines of the fugitives, spread the utmost alarm.

It was taken for granted that the fugitives must flee southwards, and accordingly Captain Blagrave proceeded with a strong party from Lahore to the Hurriki ghât (near to which Sobraon was fought); and from Umritsur, was detached in the same direction, a force (150 Punjab Infantry and some Tawana horse) under Lieutenant Boswell, a rough and ready soldier, superior to all hardships. They had to march in a drenching rain, the country nearly flooded. Sanguine hopes warmed their hearts amid the wretched weather. But, alas, for their hopes! intelligence reached the Deputy Commissioner that the mutineers had made almost due north; perhaps in hopes of getting to Cashmere, perhaps to try their luck, and by preconcerted plan to run the gauntlet of those districts in which Hindoostanee regiments, some with arms, some without arms, still existed.

Suffice it to say that it was reported at mid-day, on the 31st of July, that they were trying to skirt the left bank of the Ravee; but had met with unexpected and determined opposition from the Tehseeldar, with a posse of police, aided by a swarm of sturdy villagers at a ghât twenty-six miles from the station. A rapid pursuit was at once organized.

At four o'clock, when the district officer arrived with some eighty or ninety horsemen, he found a great struggle had taken place: the gore, the marks of the trampling of hundreds of feet, and the broken banks of the river, which, augmented with the late rains, was sweeping in a vast volume, all testified to it. Some 150 had been shot, mobbed backwards into the river, and drowned inevitably; too weakened and famished as they must have been after their forty miles flight to battle with the flood. The main body had fled upwards and swum over on pieces of wood, or floated on to an island about a mile off from the shore, where they might be descried crouching like a brood of wild fowl. It remained to capture this body, and having done so, to execute condign punishment at once.

Everything natural, artificial, and accidental, favoured the attempt and combined to secure the fate of the mutineers. So cool was the day that no horses were knocked up, though the riding was very heavy, and the distance they had made (twenty-six miles) from Umritsur was great. The sun was waxing low, and the dispirited mutineers probably would magnify the numbers of the reinforcing party; and, moreover, probably would think that the Tehseeldar, with all the villagers who had attacked them so warmly in the first instance, was still on the bank flushed with recent triumph, and eager with accession of strength; whereas, in fact, many had gone in pursuit of stragglers some ten miles off. These were the calculations of the district officer, and they turned out not amiss.

There were but two boats, both ricketty, and the boatmen unskilled. The presence of a good number of Hindoostanees among the sowars might lead to embarrassment and "accidental" escapes. The point was first how to cross this large body to the main land, if they allowed themselves to be captured at all (after the model of the fox, the geese, and the peck of oats). This was not to be done under two or three trips, without leaving two-thirds of the mutineers on the island, under too scanty a protection, and able to escape, whilst the first batch was being conveyed to the main bank; nor also without launching the first batch, when they did arrive, into the jaws of the Hindoostanee party, who in the first trip were to be left ostensibly "to take care of the horses" on the main land. From the desperate conflict which had already taken place, a considerable struggle was anticipated before these plans could be brought into operation.

The translation of the above fable to the aged Sikh Sirdar, who accompanied, and to the other heads of the pursuing party, caused intense mirth, and the plan of operations after this formula elicited general approval.

So the boats put off with about thirty sowars (dismounted of course) in high spirits; most of the Hindoostanee sowars being left on the bank. The boats straggled a little, but managed to reach the island in about twenty minutes. It was a long inhospitable patch, with tall grass; a most undesirable place to bivouac on for the night, with a rising tide; especially if wet, dispirited, hungry, without food, fire, or dry clothing. The sun was setting in golden splendour, and as the doomed men with joined palms crowded down to the shore on the approach of the boats, one side of which bristled with about sixty muskets, besides sundry revolvers and pistols, their long shadows were flung far athwart the gleaming waters. In utter despair forty or fifty dashed into the stream and disappeared, rose at a distance, and were borne away into the increasing gloom.

Some thirty or forty sowars with matchlocks (subsequently discovered to be of very precarious value) jumped into the shallow water and invested the lower side of the island, and being seen on the point of taking pot-shots at the heads of the swimmers, orders were given "not to fire." This accidental instruction produced an instantaneous effect on the mutineers. They evidently were possessed of a sudden and insane idea, that they were going to be tried by court-martial, after some luxurious refreshment. In consequence of which sixty-six stalwart sepoys submitted to be bound by a single man deputed for the purpose from the boats, and stacked like slaves in a hold into one of the two boats emptied for the purpose. Leaving some forty armed sowars on the island, and feeling certain that after the peaceful submission of the first batch (or peck of oats) the rest would follow suit and suit, orders were given to push off.

On reaching the shore, one by one, as they stepped out of the boats, all were tightly bound; their decorations and necklaces ignominiously cut off; and under guard of a posse of villagers, who had begun to assemble, and some Sikh horse, they were ordered to proceed slowly on their journey back, six miles to the police station at Ujnalla. Meanwhile the Hindoostanees (the geese) had been despatched to the island back in the boats with an overawing number of Tawana* sowars; and it was gratifying to see the

* Raised near Shahpore.

next detachment put off safely; though at one time the escorting boat got at a great distance from the escorted, and fears were entertained that escape had been premeditated. However, by dint of hallooing, with threats of a volley of musketry, the next invoice came safely to land, and were subjected to the same process of spoliation, disrobement, and pinioning. At any moment, had they made an attempt to escape, a bloody struggle must have ensued. But Providence ordered otherwise, and nothing on the side of the pursuing party seemed to go wrong. Some begged that their women and children might be spared, and were informed that the British Government did not condescend to war with women and children.

The last batch having arrived, the long straggling party were safely but slowly escorted back to the police station, almost all the road being knee-deep in water. Even this accident, by making the ground so heavy—not to mention the gracious moon, which came out through the clouds and reflected herself in myriad pools and streams, as if to light the prisoners to their fate—aided in preventing a single escape.

It was near midnight before all were safely lodged in the police station. A drizzling rain coming on prevented the commencement of the execution; so a rest until daybreak was announced. Before dawn another batch of sixty-six was brought in, and as the police station was then nearly full, they were ushered into a large round tower or bastion.

Previously to his departure with the pursuing party from Umritsur, the Deputy Commissioner had ordered out a large supply of rope, in case the numbers captured were few enough for hanging (trees being scarce), and also a reserve of fifty Sikh Levies for a firing party, in case of the numbers demanding wholesale execution; as also to be of use as a reserve in case of a fight on the island. So eager were the Sikhs that they marched straight on end, and he met them half way, twenty-three miles between the river and the police station, on his journey back in charge of the prisoners, the total number of which, when the execution commenced, amounted to 282 of all ranks, besides numbers of camp-followers, who were left to be taken care of by the villagers.

As fortune would have it, again favouring audacity, a deep dry well was discovered within one hundred yards of the police station, and its presence furnished a convenient solution as to the one remaining difficulty which was of sanitary consideration—the disposal of the corpses of the dishonoured soldiers.

The climax of fortunate coincidences seemed to have arrived when it was remembered that the 1st of August was the anniversary of the great Mahomedan sacrificial festival of the Bukra Eed. A capital excuse was thus afforded to permit the Hindoostanee Mussulman horsemen to return to celebrate it at Umritsur; while the single Christian, unembarrassed by their presence, and aided by the faithful Sikhs, might perform a ceremonial sacrifice of a different nature (and the nature of which they had not been made aware of) on the same morrow. When that morrow dawned, sentries were placed round the town, to prevent the egress of sight-seers. The officials were called; and they were made aware of the character of the spectacle they were about to witness.

Ten by ten the sepoys were called forth. Their names having been taken down in succession, they were pinioned, linked together, and marched to execution; a firing-party being in readiness. Every phase of deportment was manifested by the doomed men, after the sullen firing of volleys of distant musketry forced the conviction of inevitable death: astonishment, rage, frantic despair, the most stoic calmness. One detachment, as they passed, yelled to the solitary Anglo-Saxon magistrate, as he sat under the shade of the police station performing his solemn duty, with his native officials around him, that he, the Christian, would meet the same fate; then as they passed the reserve of young Sikh soldiery, who were to relieve the executioners after a certain period, they danced, though pinioned, insulted the Sikh religion, and called on *Gungajee* to aid them; but they only in one instance provoked a reply, which was instantaneously checked. Others again petitioned to be allowed to make one last "salaam" to the Sahib.

About 150 having been thus executed, one of the executioners swooned away (he was the oldest of the firing-party), and a little respite was allowed. Then proceeding, the number had arrived at two hundred and thirty-seven; when the district officer was informed that the remainder refused to come out of the bastion, where they had been imprisoned temporarily a few hours before. Expecting a rush and resistance, preparations were made against escape; but little expectation was entertained of the real and awful fate which had fallen on the remainder of the mutineers: they had anticipated, by a few short hours, their doom. The doors were opened, and, behold! they were nearly all dead! Unconsciously, the tragedy of Holwell's Black Hole had been re-enacted. No cries had been heard during the night, in consequence of the hubbub, tumult and shouting of the crowds of horsemen, police, tehseel guards, and excited villagers. Forty-five bodies, dead from fright, exhaustion, fatigue, heat, and partial suffocation, were dragged into light, and consigned, in common with all the other bodies, into one common pit, by the hands of the village sweepers.

One sepoy only was too much wounded in the conflict to suffer the agony of being taken to the scene of execution. He was accordingly reprieved for Queen's evidence, and forwarded to Lahore, with some forty-one subsequent captures, from Umritsur. There, in full parade before the other mutinously-disposed regiments at Meean Meer, they all suffered death by being blown away from the cannon's mouth. The execution at Ujnalla commenced at daybreak, and the stern spectacle was over in a few hours. Thus, within forty-eight hours from the date of the crime, there fell by the law nearly 500 men. All the crowds of assembled natives, to whom the crime was fully explained, considered the act "*righteous,*" but incomplete; because the magistrate did not hurl headlong into the chasm, the rabble of men, women and children, who had fled miserably with the mutineers: they marvelled at the clemency and the justice of the British.

A tumulus has been erected over the grave (already called *moofsidgar*, or rebels' hole, by the people of the vicinity), and it can be seen from a great distance; as it is on the high road, travellers ask and ponder over the tale! Hereafter the "*rebels' grave*" will be imprinted in tall capitals over the masonry in Persian, Goormookhi, and English.

The above account, written by the principal actor in the scene himself, might read strangely at home: a single Anglo-Saxon, supported by a section of Asiatics, undertaking so tremendous a responsibility, and coldly presiding over so memorable an execution, without the excitement of battle, or a sense of individual injury, to imbue the proceedings with the faintest hue of vindictiveness. The Governors of the Punjab are of the true English stamp and mould, and knew that England expected every man to do his duty, and that duty done, thanks them warmly for doing it. The crime was mutiny, and had there even been no murders to darken the memory of these men, the law was exact. The punishment was death.

Political reasons also governed the occasion, and led to the decision as to immediate execution. Nicholson had left for Delhi, and was far on his road to Loodianah. This fact was as well known to every mutinous corps as if it had been heralded trumpet-tongued through the bazaars. Nearly three months had elapsed since the first outbreak, and still Delhi was untaken. Nothing could be more gloomy than the aspect of affairs at this time. In the Doab, there were no less than seven and a half disarmed regiments, besides two armed Hindoostanee Irregulars of doubtful allegiance. Such an opportunity for an immediate and tremendous example never presented itself before, and might never do so again. To transport three hundred and twenty disciplined and desperate sepoys, after refreshing them, was almost as difficult as confining them with a due regard to safety even for so short a time; much embarrassment for escort might have been produced, and perhaps a "sensation" created among the disarmed Poorbeah regiments at Umritsur, who might have been seized with an impulse to rescue. The effect on the whole Doab, and upon the mind of native society, has not proved to have been over-estimated; for since the extinction of this regiment, there has been no "sign" among the native troops therein located. Had the 26th N. I. escaped, or even had their punishment been less terrible and instantaneous, the whole of the disarmed regiments would of a certainty have followed their example, and consequences, which it were fruitless now to speculate upon, but easy enough to conjecture, might have ensued. Their extermination probably saved the lives of thousands. In his proclamation on the subject, the Chief Commissioner wrote: "It is fervently hoped that the signal and summary punishment which has overtaken this corps, may deter all others from committing the atrocious and wanton murders which have disgraced the name of the Bengal sepoy."

Certain mock philanthropists may cry out; but with all their resolutions and orations they will never bring life back again to those that were sacrificed through the fault of the living who shrunk unreasonably from obvious and simple duty, though the performance of it might have involved circumstances of magnitude or caused sights which might tax weak nerves, and who, in closely contemplating the severity rather than the justice of the punishment, lost all sight and memory of the awful and wide catastrophes which have waited in many instances since the outbreak (as the reader may have seen), and ever will wait, in India, upon timid counsel and hesitating action.

Further on, the same rapid fate pursued the miserable residue. The gallant Major Jackson, of the 2nd Irregulars (still performing active service), went out, and pushed on so fast that he outrode his party, and encountered forty of them. He attacked, killed and wounded several, and, being in a swamp, got surrounded and wounded himself. Going further on, the desperate remnants fled by Madhopore, and Messrs. Garbett and Hanna, with the utmost gallantry (the village people being negatively loyal), dashed out and performed repeated feats of gallantry almost unaided; for which they received the merited thanks of the Government. The few remnants have since been brought in and executed. There is a well at Cawnpore, but there is also one at Ajnala!

The annexed letters are appended as a proof that no officer in the Punjab can do his duty without instant and warm recognition. They were received by the magistrate the day after the occurrences narrated. The first letter is from the chief commissioner, Sir John Lawrence, G.C.B.; the second from the next highest authority in the Punjab. They are highly characteristic, and redound to the honour of both. Their perusal will sensibly diminish the wonder why the Punjab Government is so successful.

Demi-Official from SIR JOHN LAWRENCE, K.C.B., *Chief Commissioner for the Punjaub.*

MY DEAR COOPER,— *Lahore*, 2nd *August*, 1857.

I congratulate you on your success against the 26th N. I. You and your police acted with much energy and spirit, and deserve well of the State. I trust the fate of these sepoys will operate as a warning to others. Every effort should be exerted to glean up all who are yet at large.

Roberts will no doubt leave the distribution of the rewards mainly to you. Pray see that they are allotted with due regard to merit, and that every one gets what is intended for him.

Yours sincerely,

Frederick Cooper, Esq., D.C., Umritsur. JOHN LAWRENCE.

(Copy.)

Demi-Official from ROBERT MONTGOMERY, Esq., *Judicial Commissioner for the Punjab.*

MY DEAR COOPER,— *Sunday*, 9 A.M.

All honour to you for what you have done, and right well you did it. There was no hesitation or delay, or drawing back. It will be a feather to your cap as long as you live.

Get out of the wounded man all you can, and send him to Lahore, that he may himself proclaim what has been done. The people will not otherwise believe it.

Better write an official report, and place the whole on record. Bring forward all persons who did well. Do this judiciously. I mean discriminate between the medium, the good, and the superexcellent.

Prima facie, the Tehseeldar deserves apparently great praise. Were they baulked in getting the boats? and how? Had the Tehseel people knowledge that the 26th N. I. had broken out, or did they first ascertain it on seeing them?

You will have abundant money to reward all, and the (executioners) Sikhs should have a good round sum given to them.

I congratulate you very heartily on your success. There will be some stragglers; have them all picked up, and any you get send *us* now. You have had slaughter enough. We want a few for the troops here, and also for evidence.

Believe me, yours sincerely,

F. Cooper, Esq., D.C. R. MONTGOMERY.

P.S.—The other three regiments here were very shaky yesterday, but I hardly think they will now go. I wish they would, as they are a nuisance; and not a man would escape if they do.—R. M.

Lord Canning, who, through evil report and good report, has steadily insisted on discriminating justice, at once accorded his high commendation of the summary proceedings narrated in this chapter.

Letters received by the Author from the Rajah of Kuppoorthulla.

My Dear Mr. Cooper,— *Jullundur, 9th July*, 1857.

In these days of peril and difficulties those who are acquainted with each other should be nearer to each by writing occasionally. You know how often we are misled by wicked and designed men by false reports. True news in these days are a great blessing. How much we look for and read with real gratification the brief circular issued by the Judicial Commissioner. My object is simply to inform myself with the affairs of things as going on in your district as well as your own personal welfare, which is of great importance to me.

I am quite confident and so is my people about me, that the troubles will soon have an end. Delhi will be taken, the rebels will be punished, and peace will be established without much bloodshed or delay.

Hoping you are quite well in this trying weather,

Yours very sincerely,

F. H. Cooper, Esq. Rundheer Sing, *Rajah.*

My Dear Mr. Cooper,— *Jullundur, 4th August*, 1857.

I consider it a fit occasion to drop a line or two in the way of congratulating you for the triumphant return you have made of the disarmed mutinous sepoys of 26th N. I. . . . . . .

You have certainly made a very good impression on the mind of all the disaffected troops in Punjab. I hear very frequently from my own people, who had occasion to wait on you, that you have, invariably kind to them, never failed to produce that effect on their as well as my mind, which is so pleasing to a native of this country. I have lately received a letter from Shahabuddeen, one of my tehseeldars on business at Umritsur, says that you have been very kind to him. This is to pray for the prosperity of the English officers.

I remain yours most sincerely,

F. Cooper, Esq. RUNDHEER SING, *Rajah.*

MY DEAR MR. COOPER,— *Kuppoorthulla, October*, 1857.

I have no doubt you must have considered me very rude in not doing myself the pleasure of congratulating you on the fall of Delhi, but I assure you I was so much pressed for time, that I was obliged to confine myself to such letters as were most emergent, and even those got through great difficulty.

You know that I have been so long in Jullundur; and the work here was entirely stopped, on account of my not being here.

We most sincerely congratulate you on the fall of Delhi, which we longed for; and we hope the country all around will soon be settled; and we should very much like to hear the mutineers getting a good lesson for their deeds, which I hope will shortly commence. Trusting you are in the best of health, with regards,

Yours very sincerely,

F. H. Cooper, Esq. RUNDHEER SING, *Rajah.*

CHAPTER VII.

MUTINIES AT FEROZEPORE AND PESHAWUR.

In every great crisis certain terms attain a familiar significance, from their meaning a great deal more than their import in ordinary acceptation would warrant. Every one knows what pregnant meaning a "difficulty" has in America. So in the Punjab, the words "accounted for" and "disposed of" have universally attained pertinent significance. In the last chapter it was shown how the 26th were both "accounted for" and "disposed of." The present will show how the 10th Light Cavalry, though "accounted for," were not "disposed of" at Ferozepore; and how the 51st N. I. were both accounted for and disposed of in the most complete sense of the term at Peshawur.

The first occurrence will prove how watchful and wily an enemy we deal with in the Asiatic. He studies all our habits, adapts himself to all our vagaries, and almost fathoms our thoughts. As in the great design of the insurrection, so in the petty scheme of the rise of the 10th Cavalry, the most advantageous hour was seized. It is just possible that the escape of the 26th N. I. (though not their fate) had met their ears; or that the news had reached them that their horses (for they had been dismounted) were to be taken away. However, they broke loose on the 10th of August, and attempted to seize the guns, which had been posted on the open space between the European Infantry barracks and the south face of the fort. The hour chosen was the dinner hour. They killed the sergeant at the guns, and wounded several others, jumped on their horses, and galloped all over the place. They must have been but carelessly disarmed, as they were sufficiently provided with swords, pistols, and spears.

Major Marsden, the deputy commissioner, galloped over to provide for contingencies, and was at once attacked by a trooper. Both horses were unmanageable, and flashes only were interchanged; but Marsden's pistol, however, took effect on a companion of the trooper. All families were cared for, and during the interval of great confusion, the Patialah Horse, some Levies, and the 1st Bombay Fusiliers were being collected. Meanwhile the mutineers jumped on all available horses bare-backed, and galloped through cantonments. They had captured momentarily the guns, and were advancing to turn them on the barracks, when the depôt of the 61st and the artillery rushed up and retook them before they could fire.

The splendid and determined resistance of the artillery guard, against the first shock of such tremendous odds, was worthy of the British soldier. Private Molony was nearly hacked to pieces, and since died. A young gunner saved a Corporal Doherty's life at the expense of two severe wounds, and in return was rescued by the Corporal. The complicity of the syce drivers is undoubted; their horses were left in the most convenient state to be let loose by the mutineers, and the accoutrements and harness had been taken to pieces, ostensibly for cleaning purposes, but unmistakably that the utmost delay might occur, and the mutineers be allowed to get away. And over such men, and in the teeth of such facts, the regular courts-martial have been sitting!

A most unaccountable error occurred in the management of a gun placed originally to command a bridge leading from the barracks to the native infantry. It was fired into the rows of cavalry horses, and while it hardly disturbed the mutineers, killed and wounded thirty-two horses! Fifty-nine horses were made away with by the mutineers. Many officers' chargers besides were stolen; the mutineers being bent more on flight than aught else. They signalized their flight, however, by dastardly murdering their veterinary surgeon, Mr. Nelson, a talented and much-regretted officer. It is said the poor fellow lost his stirrup, and received a sword cut on the back of his head and neck, which knocked him off his horse, when some felon assassin gashed his throat from ear to ear as he lay on the ground.

The sowars rode about collecting horses, ponies, and native arms from every one they met; also hog-spears, saddlery, and every weapon they could find in officers' bungalows: it was fortunate that the officers were absent. Some dashed to the kutcherry compound in hopes of treasure, but were immediately repulsed by the Sikh guard. Fourteen officers' horses were stolen, valued at nearly twenty thousand rupees. Two hundred sowars thus having replenished themselves, escaped by a road down which no artillery could follow, and, as a matter of course, distanced all infantry pursuit. Major Marsden, however, recovered the carriage of General Van Cortlandt. It will be gathered from the above narrative that the guns were completely surprised.

Previously to the outbreak the cavalry had despatched a great part of their families toward Sirsa on hackeries by the jungle roads. Had more officers accompanied Major Marsden with the Patialah horse, they might have harassed the rear of the retreating party, and perhaps the infantry could have come up.

A very different drama was enacted a week after this at Peshawur; where the military arrangements, from first to last, under General Cotton have elicited universal admiration. A second search for concealed arms in the 51st N. I. lines being deemed necessary, Captain Bartlett, commanding the 28th Punjab Infantry (one of the newly-raised corps), was deputed to that duty. The work occupied longer time than was expected; and the noon-day gun had fired, and still the lines of two companies remained for search. When of a sudden the whole regiment rose and rushed upon Captain Bartlett, Lieutenant Roberts, and Ensign Platt. The first escaped almost by a miracle from his assailants, after receiving a severe mauling. He rushed into a tank, drew his revolver, and kept his assailants at bay. Ensign Platt, quite a youth, wrestled with a man in the water, and was tossed into a shallow well. The pistol of Lieutenant Roberts twice missed fire, and he was knocked down three times successively.

The 18th could not open fire until the recruits had extricated themselves from the huts, and from among the mutineers with whom they were mixed up. The first volley was decisive; some fifty mutineers immediately fell; numbers were bayoneted in the lines; the rest fled indiscriminately,—some towards the barracks and magazine of the Peshawur Light Horse, whence they were immediately repulsed with severe loss; others for the lines of the 18th, where they were at once made prisoners, as were a third party in the peach gardens by the same loyal and energetic corps. Those who attempted to flee through the Sudder Bazaar were pursued, and nearly all cut up by the eager soldiers of the 70th and 27th Regiments.

Foiled at all points, the main body ran away towards Jumrood, still closely followed by the 18th infantry in skirmishing order. The Deputy-Commissioner, Captain James, was early in the field with his Mooltanee Horse, and had soon cut up fifty fugitives. Another party of Mooltanees, attached to the Peshawur Light Horse, under Lieutenant Gosling, soon killed fifteen or twenty, besides making thirty-seven prisoners. The pursuing force was overpowering and determined, and the result was almost complete annihilation of the mutineers with, as will be seen, the most trivial loss, and that principally from the burning sun. The pursuit by the 18th Punjab Infantry was especially long, keen, and close. Standing crops were beat up, ravines probed, as if for pheasants and hares, and with great success. The conduct of the 18th Punjab Native Infantry deserved every encomium. Some idea may be gathered of the terrific and swift destruction, when it is remembered that the strength of the regiment before the mutiny amounted to 871. The Punjab Infantry shot and killed 125; Captain James's party killed 40; Lieutenant Gosling's party killed 15. The Peshawur Light Horse, the villagers, and H. M.'s 27th and 70th killed 36. By sentence of drum-head court-martial, on the same day, there were executed by H. M.'s 87th, 187; and by a similar summary tribunal, on the 29th of August, 167; also on the same date, 84; one thanahdar killed five: total, within about 30 hours after the mutiny, no less than 659! There were also 110 in confinement. One sepoy literally died two deaths, and the first time was buried: when the fatal volley was discharged he fell with the others, and feigned death; his body was flung rather high up in the chasm, and covered over with lime. He managed to crawl out at dark, and escape to the hills; but was caught and brought in. He pleaded previous demise;

but ineffectually, and this time he moulders with the forms of his mutinous comrades.

There were but four deaths in action among the pursuing party, and three from sun-stroke; the latter including Lieutenant-Colonel Cooper.

The Divisional Order, published by Brigadier-General Cotton, is an interesting document.

Division Head-Quarters, Peshawur, 2nd Sept.

No. 420.—The recent outbreak *en masse* of the soldiers of the 51st N. I. brings another corps on the long list of those, which, after years of gallantry and meritorious services, have basely revolted against the Government, and on no occasion throughout has retribution more speedily and thoroughly awaited the mutiny and treachery of these misguided men.

2. Terrible, indeed, has been the example made of this formerly-esteemed and highly-disciplined corps. In a few hours the 51st N.I., which had faithfully served the State for half a century, and proudly bore on its colours the words Punniar, Punjab, Mooltan, and Goojerat, ceased to exist, and those colours have been put out of sight for ever.

3. Prompt and sure has been, and ever will be, the punishment awarded in the Peshawur garrison to the perpetrators of atrocious crimes. Mutineers and deserters must suffer the extreme penalty of the law, and let these just and fearful examples be solemn warnings for the future.

4. To the loyal, true, and well-affected of Her Majesty's and the Honourable Company's forces under his command, who on many trying occasions and throughout have evinced the most determined and energetic bearing, Brigadier-General Cotton tenders his warmest thanks. At the recent mutiny the conduct of the troops was most exemplary. The heat was excessive, many valuable men in the discharge of their duty were laid low by an overpowering sun.

5. The best thanks of the Brigadier-General are especially

due, and they are warmly given to Brigadier Galloway, commanding the Peshawur district, and to Colonel Chute, of H. M.'s 70th Regiment, and Lieutenant-Colonel Kyle, of H. M.'s Enniskillens, commanding wings of the Peshawur Brigade, as well as to the whole staff and regimental officers employed on a service of very considerable difficulty.

Immediately subsequent to these events, the whole of the sepoy lines not occupied by the newly-raised Punjab regiments were levelled by commissariat elephants, and the sepoys themselves were marched into camp with the artillery pointed on them.

And since the discovery of concealed arms, all the native regiments (but the still armed 21st) are stationed under guns and watched, as at Lahore, and the slightest move will be the signal of a storm of iron hail.

CHAPTER VIII.

DELHI.

THIS narrative professes to contain an account of the principal events which happened in the Punjab up to the fall of Delhi. The reconquest of the imperial city was, however, accomplished almost wholly and entirely by Punjab forces. History will hereafter do ample justice to the heroic endurance of the tenfold more than Crimean sufferings of the European officers and men, though unaggravated by Crimean incapacities: history will place the chaplet on the brows of those heroes who toiled, from the victorious General Wilson down to the lowest soldiers, under a tropical sun; who conquered in thirty fierce battles with a disciplined, overpowering, and savage enemy; and who gloriously and finally vindicated the supremacy and the honour of Great Britain, by unfurling the flag of England on the walls of Delhi.

All European India was impatient to hear of the

capture of Delhi from the moment that, under General Sir H. Barnard, the first original defeat of the rebels had taken place. With scant information, the superhuman difficulties against which the force had to contend were inadequately appreciated.

A month had nearly elapsed between the original outbreak, and the arrival of the army before Delhi. The interval was employed by the mutineers in vast preparations; and almost daily accessions to their strength had been made. They had been joined by the Rohilcund, the Neemuch, and the Nusseerabad brigades. Troops from the Saugor and Nerbudda territories, and detached mutinous corps from various stations in the provinces had arrived; and as they arrived were invariably ordered out, to measure their strength against the British force. This lent a degree of pertinacity and an appearance of sustained vigour to their attacks, which sensibly diminished when the last accession had arrived and had experienced their first lesson at British hands.

In rigid accuracy, the British force before Delhi were the beseiged, and not the besiegers; and from the relative strength of the armies, the position occupied, the impossibility of a complete investment of a city seven miles in circumference, it could not be otherwise. A seventh only of the line of investment could be held by our troops, when General Wilson assumed command on the retirement of General Reed. And as the remaining six-sevenths were in possession of the mutinous garrison, the position was assailable, and assailed (though invariably followed by disgraceful defeat) by the enemy in front, in the flank, and the rear simultaneously. The environs of the city, too, were peculiarly favourable for the description of fighting, or secure assassination policy; in which the sepoys proved themselves but too destructive. They abounded, as the vicinities of all imperial cities do, with relics of ancient palaces, ruined tombs, deserted mosques, serais, walled gardens filled with dense shrubbery and large trees, amid which the enemy flitted about like wasps. Besides this, there was every species of harsh undulating surface and broken ridge almost impracticable for cavalry, and affording the utmost facilities for concealment and surprise. To decimate the Europeans; to exasperate them by this kind of attack; to bribe them by feints into the open, and lead them into ambuscade, was the aim of the sepoy leaders.

With an efficient siege train and an investment of the line with some 25,000 men, Delhi could not have stood a fortnight, as the fortifications are not of formidable character. On ordinary calculation the enemy inside could not number less than from forty to fifty thousand fighting men; half trained and disciplined by ourselves; men accustomed to the habits of Europeans, and dangerously aware of their peculiar weakness: as dangerously aware also of their peculiar and unmatched power; inasmuch as they never fought them in fair pitched battle after the first.

There is, we believe, no parallel in the annals of warfare to the position of Major-General Wilson when he assumed command of the indomitable little band before Delhi on the 20th July. His base of operations unsafe; European troops almost the only troops reliable; treachery rife in his own camp; diseases on the increase: the numerical force at his command (exclusive of small bodies of cavalry and artillery), consisting only of about 2,200 Europeans and 1,500 natives, in all 3,700 bayonets; while the enemy were literally numberless, in perfect preparation behind strong defences, and perfectly equipped.

This was not all. Our own magazines had supplied the enemy's force with one hundred and fourteen field pieces, with sixty field pieces manned by our own trained gunners, and Sikh infantry trained to the gun drill, who exhibited (to our loss) the excellent practice they had acquired. In all probability none of the same class will be permitted to attain any such dangerous efficiency again. Even in a military point of view, against a garrison so desperate, so strongly armed, and with religion for their war cry, any attack would have met with fierce resistance. To a certainty, the British camp and hospitals, if left undefended, would have been attacked and destroyed, and their baggage would have fallen into the enemy's hands.

Supposing any bold attempt at escalading the city walls had been made, failure would have been attended with calamity not usual in ordinary warfare. The Government was engaged ostensibly in the easy task, according to all precedent (as long as the impression of invincibility was abroad), of punishing its rebellious subjects with the strong arm of power: but the strong arm of power had become a shadow. Honour and prestige were at stake when Lord Raglan was before Sebastopol, had he been forced to retire to his ships. An empire, and lasting dishonour were at stake, when General Wilson held his ground magnificently before Delhi; resting his hopes of succour on the consummate political wisdom, determination, and foresight of Sir John Lawrence, and his hopes of success on the indomitable courage of the British soldier. The position was critical; reinforcements strong and speedy were imperative; and reliance on the Chief Commissioner was justly reposed.*

Within two days after General Wilson had applied for reinforcements, he was informed that the Kumaon Battalion (Ramsay's), 400 strong, had already passed Loodianah, and would be at Delhi on the 4th of August; that H. M.'s 52nd, 600 bayonets (fresh from the victory at Trimmoo ghât), military police, 400 bayonets; Mooltanee Horse, 200, and a nine-pounder battery had been also ordered down; the whole under the command of Brigadier-General Nicholson. These would all arrive by the 15th of August. Furthermore—regardless of all lesser risks when all was staked on the great game, and the fate of India was trembling in the balance—the Chief Commissioner made arrangements for the despatch of the 2nd Punjab Infantry (Captain Green's), 700; H.M.'s 61st, 400; wing of Belooch (Colonel Farquhar's), 500; 4th Punjab Infantry, 400 (Captain Wilde): two Companies H.M.'s 8th, one detachment of H.M.'s 8th, 200; and Dawes's troop of Horse Artillery 100—in all 2,000 men.

* To retire upon Kurnaul would have been political suicide.

General Wilson felt invigorated. Four thousand trained and brave troops were coming to his relief. Until their arrival, his policy was to bide his time and repulse attack; all his energies were exerted, therefore, to prevent undue waste of life, and his exertions were crowned with complete success. Never had appeared a single complaint (though the freest spoken letters were admitted into the papers) against any commissariat arrangements; and the Government of the Cis-Sutlej States, by Mr. G. C. Barnes—who, literally, by his moral influence maintained the security of the base of operations by ensuring the co-operation of the chiefs in keeping open the line of communication—left nothing to fear. The indefatigable Mr. Ricketts, at Loodianah, had called into existence, out of a naked country, almost magical aid for transports, and laid the General commanding under a debt of thanks he munificently repaid.

The Rajah of Jheend had given peculiar and uncalled-for evidence of his allegiance and devotion. About the middle of July, when nothing could exceed the gloomy aspect of affairs (though, had the British power been temporarily vanquished in the desperate struggle, he must infallibly have been obliterated for his acts, yet) he volunteered a letter to the Chief

Commissioner deprecating doubts, pledging himself to aid, and assuring him that he was in the cause heart and hand. Throughout he was anxious that his troops should share in the assault of Delhi. Nobly has he redeemed his pledge. Not otherwise so, the Maharajah of Pattiala; but his realm is large; its confines dangerously contiguous, and open to infection from the Delhi districts. About this period he solicited a private interview with Mr. G. C. Barnes, and frankly asked him if in his own opinion the British Government would pull through, as the horizon looked so lowering. The Commissioner affected to think, drew a piece of paper towards him, and, after show of elaborate calculation, apprised the Maharajah that if the State could hold out until the 30th of August all was safe; and it would be stronger than ever. The Maharajah departed highly pleased, and redoubled his efforts.

Foreseeing the value of assuring the loyalty of native chiefs by exhibiting the Maharajah Goolab Singh of Cashmere in active co-operation and cordial alliance, Sir John Lawrence demanded a contingent; and the demand was acceded to, on faithful construction of the international engagements between feudatory chieftains and the paramount power. But, as if to test again the mental resources of the local

Government, and to offer a crowning evidence of its mastery in unravelling political complications, the Maharajah died. Doubts were then entertained, not unreasonably, as to the internal state of Cashmere. The prestige and capacity of the father was lost to us; but the want of them might be advantageous to us in the son. Sharing by repute much of his father's cunning, and, perhaps, more of his unscrupulousness, Runbeer Singh was not yet seated firmly on the throne. Rajah Jowahir Singh had afforded the Government effectual aid in the crisis; and the late Maharajah's conduct towards him had not met with approval. The counterpoise was in sight of the young king; the contingent, therefore, proceeded on its journey to the seat of war. Sinister reports had been spread, about Cashmere having been the refuge for destitute mutineers now, and the 66th N.I. disbanded eight years' since by Sir Charles Napier.

The conduct of the late Maharajah had been not altogether without suspicion in the crisis. Half the contingent were reported to be composed of Poorbeeahs. More than the reverse, however, turned out to be the case: nearly all were Dogras and Rajpoots. The ubiquitous Chief Commissioner himself met them at Jullundur, gave them a reception, confirmed them in their loyalty by an assuring address; adverted to the invariable custom of the British Government of pensioning the families of those who had fallen in war; distributed robes of honour to the superior officers, and largess to the men, and ushered them, thus pecuniarily and mentally reinvigorated, to their destitution. Thus the last card had been played

The capture of Delhi had become the turning point of our fate. Into the sink of the vile city all the scum of India had gathered. To act on the defensive, unless the defensive action was accompanied by incessant punishment of the mutineers, was becoming tenfold more dangerous as the days wore on. The Bombay army was at least shaky, and no tidings of troops coming out *overland* reached the anxious ear of the Chief Commissioner. From Bombay up to this time, the first detachment only of a single European regiment had arrived. The most loyally disposed began to quaver: the storm might burst on every quarter at once.

Sir John Lawrence (himself in former days Magistrate of Delhi), acquainted with every nook and corner of its streets, assured in his own mind, and by the light of his own vast experience, of the double game every Asiatic plays, especially with divided interests, as in this crisis, felt that the time for the final blow had now come. Like Wellington at Waterloo, he shut up his telescope. The mutiny in the Bengal Presidency had arrived at its worst, and the dark lane had arrived at its turning. No fresh arrival of mutineers was to be expected in Delhi for the present, and the Gwalior mutineers were far off. Social disorganisation was complete in the interior of the city: the house was divided against itself, and was now to fall. Never, with all their vast resources, had the enemy made any sensible impression on the British Army of Delhi.

All possible reinforcements had been scraped together, even to the risk of self-sacrifice. Every day now had become fraught with danger: even our prestige was waning. Sikhs had come back to the Punjab and declared they were fighting "our" battles. One old Sikh had thought it just as likely they might be fighting against us in a year hence! The subordinate Presidencies of Madŕas and Bombay (the latter especially) held together with difficulty, but with the utmost wisdom and bravery, were all awaiting the fate of Delhi. The frontier, though guarded by an Edwardes and a Cotton, might, on the death of Dost Mahomed, who was old and ill, be invaded by twenty thousand Affghans.

Fever, as usual, had laid its unrelenting and

prostrating hand upon the European soldiery of the Peshawur valley. Hardly eleven hundred men were fit for active duty; although there were from five to six thousand disarmed Poorbeeah regiments to watch. All these considerations pointed to prompt action. Delhi was to be taken now or never. The British Government was fairly at bay. Never was the want of railways and steam flotillas more keenly deplored. Reinforcements from the south had long been given up as hopeless, although the most confident predictions had been promulgated. Even the detention, inactive, of so preponderating a native contingent before Delhi, though friendly for the time, was to be deprecated; and it was as well that they had as little leisure to "think" as possible. The insurrection of Googara almost immediately after the capture of Delhi indicated ominously how near the point of durance had been stretched. Peshawur was waxing more feverish every day, and Edwardes grew anxious. Six per cent. Government paper was twenty-five per cent. discount. Lahore and Umritsur were equally excited. The Bombay presidency was beginning to disbelieve our power, and tottered sensibly.

The final blow was preceded by a brilliant victory under the lamented General Nicholson. Almost immediately on his arrival with the reinforcements, previously detailed, he was moved out by Wilson to attack, at a place called Nujjuffghur, a large force of the rebels, who had hoped to get into our rear, cut off our communications, and capture our siege train. This force was composed of the Kotah and Neemuch mutineers. Though so obvious a piece of strategy had suggested itself to General Bukht Khan, yet, to our inestimable advantage, it was providentially never attempted.

Nicholson was famous for his marches, and again, with the country under water, he appeared at the right spot at the right time. The enemy fell into the jaws of the lion. He attacked them, cut them up, captured all their guns, completely routed the force, and ended by demolishing a bridge which formed a most important communication. Every arrangement was, as might be expected under such a commander, admirable. It was the only aggressive stroke we had been enabled to make, and the depressing effect on the mutineers was electric; for it was the first time they had essayed anything but sorties. The force returned. The bands played, and almost the whole army of Delhi turned out to greet the victors.

While this engagement was lasting, the insurgents, under the impression that General Wilson had left himself weak in camp, ventured out, and attacked the position in force, and with the usual results. No impression was made; they suffered great loss, and the British army showed a very slender list of casualties.

The assault and fall of Delhi is matter for the historian, and will furnish hereafter volumes of the deepest interest, filled with the most extraordinary details of British foresight, stoic courage, endurance of privation, and brilliant instances of chivalry unapproached in the stories of war. Has any artillery officer in warfare been able to perform his duty with ordinary cheerfulness when finding shell after shell, though most carefully laid, fall far beyond, or short of the mark, or when he listened perhaps for the explosion was rewarded with silence? And why? The fuses were found purposely reduced to irregular lengths; treacherous, though trusted native hands filled shells with sand instead of powder; the charges of powder were carefully increased or diminished by the same felon agency, so as to disconcert the besiegers. Have water-carriers ever in the history of war been treacherously furnished with strong drink instead of water, by an enemy, so as to intoxicate the senses they could not subdue? These, and thousands of other treacheries, which the British mind was soon taught to realise, will hereafter come to light. Nor will the position of the Commander in such a peculiar emergency be lost sight of.

Demoralisation after the capture and sack of a large city is a temporary and inevitable evil, but eventual subjection to proper control is generally to be calculated upon; in this case it was scarcely certain, and the utmost precautions were taken. Half of General Nicholson's force was composed of new levies, besides Sikh and Goorkha corps; who, although trained and perfectly disciplined, were inflamed with hereditary hatred, eager for their long-deferred plunder, and exasperated by the protracted conflict. Even the feelings of the British troops had been aroused to a pitch of excitement which might temporarily threaten discipline, and certainly endanger loss. A succession of street conflicts might almost decimate those against whom the principal fire was sure to be aimed; for though the non-combatants of the city, and thousands of residents who had not taken arms, might desert, the remainder, it was known, would fight with the fanaticism of despair. It was wonderful that a spark of ardour was left to the European after the long exposure and incessant conflicts of the preceding four months. Such are some of the very anomalous and peculiar disadvantages with which our commanders had to contend.

The enemy, however, were not without treachery in their own camp. Equally difficult was it for them to know friend from foe. The British were furnished with an intelligence department as trustworthy as their own. Notwithstanding the storm of calamities, which to all external appearances had well nigh overwhelmed the State, there were not wanting thousands of far-seers who felt that, the first shock having been withstood, the day of sweeping, simultaneous insurrection had gone by for another century, and that the grappling-irons of Great Britain upon Hindustan were scarcely loosened, and were about to be fixed more firmly than ever.

Among these wise and far-seeing men was the Meer Moonshee of the late Sir H. Lawrence, Rujjub Ali. Almost before the end of June an espionage and intelligence department of extraordinary value was organized, through Asiatic agents, under the guidance principally of Lieutenant Hodson. It is within our power to record briefly hereafter the main incidents only of the assault on Delhi; but the interior of the city could be vividly imagined from the almost daily bulletins furnished by the spies.

A veil must be drawn over the horrors which

inaugurated the brief and bloody attempt at rule of the last of the Moguls. "The civilization of fifty-three years," wrote a newswriter to the Rajah of Kuppoorthullah, "has been destroyed in three hours." A reality of that scarcely shadowed in dreams of bygone ages, was being enacted. Glitter, squalor, mock monarchy, lip subserviency, license, fanaticism, bloodshed, treachery, cruel murders, confiscation, pillage, abject cowardice, jealousies, strifes, vacillation, disorganization, and finally hopeless barbarism characterized the state of things in the city during the revolt. Having no wish to harrow unnecessarily the feelings of the reader, a few only of the salient points will be touched upn.

Early in the insurrection a bunniah wrote what must have been passing in the mind of every respectable native. "If Delhi is taken quickly there remains no other fear; if not, this is a time to be anxious for our lives and property. The price of gold mohurs has risen to twenty-four rupees."

On the 2nd of June *not a European remained alive!* The extraordinary excitement of fanaticism was found necessary even in the earliest stage to give the selfish and trembling sepoy a religious "cry." "Moulvies" especially flocked to Delhi and became Ghazees, and devoted themselves to the slaughter of the infidels. The green standard waved over the Jumma Musjid, and attracted all eyes. The dread of British might and vengeance was manifest from the first; so no attempt was made to come out on the Kurnaul road, though preparations for defence were actually adopted. Rumours of collusion with Affghanistan were rife, although no direct communication seems to have been opened; but the mutiny of all the Poorbeeah regiments was confidently relied on from the first. The King, or those who used his name and influence, proclaimed the remission of revenue to all villagers who joined. Meanwhile the army before Delhi was kept aware of the position of all the guns inside, and of the mutinous reinforcements.

The pulsation of politics appears to have been nicely distinguished. Sometimes we read "The King is dispirited at the result of the last fight, and wishes to retreat, or to cross the river." The Mahajuns had been asked to advance twenty lakhs; but they requested some sort of government, and the resumption of the "ordinary routine of trade" as a guarantee.

The twenty-second attack had been made on the little army when General Wilson assumed command. On the 19th of July it was known that "a Kerannie" (subsequently proved to be a Sergeant-Major of the rebel 28th N. I.) had joined, and was working with the Bareilly mutinous brigade. Further items of intelligence, of sufficient significance, continued to pour in. Disorganization had begun reigning in the city. The King had proclaimed pensions of three rupees monthly to the widows whose husbands fell in his cause. Seven men had been killed in an affray originating in a cow-slaying enterprise; confusion and riot ensued, and the sepoys, not the King, were "dominant." The released Agra gaol convicts had begun to come in; desertion of sepoys, who had provided themselves with gold mohurs had become not unfrequent. There was no care for the wounded: there was no lint or ointment, as in British days, for open sores. The amount of percussion caps had been narrowly counted, and was said to be failing. The plan of fighting the British force every day did not appear to "succeed;" and arrangements for a grand assault, with the King at the head of the army and the whole city population, was determined upon, but not carried out. A subadar of artillery, named Bukht Khan, had been named Commander-in-Chief; from personal preponderance, only, apparently. He and others had represented to the King that the Delhi and Meerut forces were too fond of plunder, and objected to fighting. Three divisions had been made, and a General created to go out at each attack!

Sometimes news almost diverting was communicated. Poets sprang forth. One of the earliest emanations of their muse was the following. It possibly has lost somewhat of the pith in the translation, which is as follows:—

> "Suraj-ood-deen Bahadoor, the conqueror of England,
> Second of his name, has issued a new currency."

Horrid intelligence, however, predominated; gratifying to the debased, sensual and cruel Asiatic, but almost paralysing to the English mind. The British troops required not the aid of exasperated feelings and factitious incitements to urge them to do their duty; so the tales of Jhansi and Cawnpore were kept from them, out of respect to their feelings.

Again, a Pundit rich in occult lore had made his appearance, and had declared, by his knowledge of the stars, that the sepoys would rule this year in India! Tuesday the 21st of July was the day this oracle fixed for the great attack. "The horses' hoofs were to be steeped in blood, and the action was to rival the great conflict of the Maha Bharut; after that the sepoys were to be dominant over India."

Pursuing the rather tangled thread of native information from the interior, we find other important and pregnant indications. "The rebels" (even on the 19th of July,) "were getting sick of ill success, and some escaped every day in disguise." Indeed after the assault, it was found that the majority of those who defended the city were armed fanatics and townspeople.

The necessity also of hospitals began to dawn upon the new authorities at Delhi, and native doctors, a class who have as a rule behaved disgracefully, were found to dress wounds. Up to this date our small artillery force had made but little impression on the city. Hopes were still entertained by the King of the monetary aid of native chieftains; such as the rebel Nawab of Jujjur, who has since been hanged. Fairly accurate information continued to be obtained, even up to the numbers killed by the British army in every repulse; and the repulses were not only signal but invariable. For days and weeks the gallantry of the 9th Lancers, of the Artillery, of the renowned 60th Rifles, and of officers and men whose names are familiar as household words, was the theme of admiration in all peaceful quarters.

From between the fifteenth to the end of July the fate of India was in the balance. The most tremendous efforts of the mutineers were directed against the British at this period, and with fearful odds. Our Asiatic spies were vigilant. Every reinforcement to the mutineers was carefully detailed; and every engineering project explained, even to the length and width of beams of wood in contemplated structures.

One of the most leading characters appears to have been the aforenamed Subadár Bukht Khan, upon whom the King conferred the rank and title of General. He is described by his late commanding officer (Captain Waddy, H.A.), to have been "sixty years of age; to have served the Company for forty years; his height about five feet ten inches; forty-four inches round the chest; family of Hindoo extraction, but converted under temptation of territorial acquisition; a very bad rider, owing to large stomach and round thighs, but clever, and a good drill." Such is a faithful and authentic description of one of the rebel leaders. The Neemuch force, when it arrived on the 27th of July, did not approve of this gentleman being Commander-in-Chief; and splits in council, most valuable to our cause, began to widen into breaches of internal disunion. Even the varied and continual, though unauthentic stories of large reinforcements of Europeans from the south, while they afforded occasional and spasmodic exultation to British hearts, contributed not a little to the dismay of the rebels, from their very vagueness. The native mind actuated upon by fear is especially prone to exaggeration and loss of self-reliance.

The fame of General Neill at Allahabad and Cawnpore had not been too glowingly depicted; and the anticipated arrival of two European regiments, called respectively the "devils" and the "cannibals," was deplored by the inhabitants of Delhi. These regiments of enviable fame were supposed to be the Madras Fusiliers and the 93rd Highlanders. In short, the hopes of the British, even in ultimate reinforcements, never came up to the fabulous credulity of the natives in their awful proximity.

About the 31st of July we heard of premeditated attacks postponed in consequence of the Commander-in-Chief, Bukht Khan, and General Ghous Khan hating one another. On the great Bukra Eed, as on other religious occasions, the utmost fanaticism was incited in place of bravery. But, except among the local Goojur population, sympathy was scarce throughout the country. General Wilson's policy of repulsing with effect, and leaving the mutineers to fight amongst themselves, told well. Unaware of our line of policy, though strongly convinced of the indomitable determination of the British, no endeavours were omitted after the last day of July to seduce our troops into isolated positions; but these never succeeded, through great demonstrations were attempted.

True to Asiatic system, the mutineers, cowed by

incessant losses, notwithstanding their numerical preponderance, and disheartened by the conflict of selfish internal feeling as to their future destiny, began to assail the King, as responsible for not having succeeded in the position in which they had placed him. They complained of want of support, after retiring night after night discomfited. The King replied that the mutineers had ruined him; whereupon he was railed at in full durbar. The King's son, the master-spirit of the rebellion, though stained with the slaughter of innocents, found it impossible to govern the malcontent spirits of the black-hearted soldiers; violent reproaches were exchanged, and delays in making attacks were petitioned for, which perforce had to be granted. These delays were of fruitful value to General Wilson and his army. In the city, the standing army was beginning to be found "unwieldy, and funds ran short." More attempts, therefore, to cut off British supplies were again made; but in no case succeeded. The British mind had been frequently cheered by reports of the enemy's want of percussion caps, but the well-informed knew that at least three hundred thousand and more must be in store. Experiments were essayed at making detonating powder, and with signal failure. The most urgent attempts were made to seduce the Maharajah of Pattialah, and to impress upon the people the triumph of the rebel cause. But it came to the ears of the King, on the authority of "Toolla Ram, that the English were not yet driven into the sea." He had made incessant demands on the city. He had even been importuned to send subsidies to Waleedad Khan, the miscreant of Malagurh.

By the 4th of August desertions from the mutineers became of daily occurrence, especially under pretence of "furlough." That reinforcements were pouring down from the Punjab was no secret to them, and the name of Lawrence was dismaying. The Ghazees (fanatics) who arrived were also a source of trouble to the King's party, as their politics on the 4th of August had swerved considerably towards the English side. About the 5th of August a General Bukhtawur Khan (probably Bukht Khan) seems to have got into disgrace; for we hear that through his neglect the force of General Sirdar Singh had "got out of spirits; they had been kept in the wet for two days." This disagreement the King is said to have reconciled. The hearts of the most sanguine rebels still entertained hopes of succour from Gwalior; but none came. Though there was no famine in the city, there was much disease. Prices were still low, but cholera began to rage.

The citizens almost asked to be rescued from sepoy rule. Friday was an especial day for sorties; but Baal did not answer to the call of his priests. Rohilcund affairs, about the beginning of August, seemed to have occupied the King's attention; and he had hopes that residents of the Gangetic Doab, who pretended to be eager to pay revenue on arrival of his Majesty's chupprassies, might be induced to remit money.

Occasionally the King dallied with the muse, and the translation of one couplet runs thus—"I, Nuffer (his poetical name), will seize London; for what is the distance from Hindoostan?" The King was also informed from Lucknow that Goordutoola Beg, son of Mendoo Khan, had reinstated the son of Wajid Allee Shah, late King of Oude, subject to the Emperor's approval, and had commenced coining with the following inscription:—

> "Bazar zud sicca nusrut tarazee,
> Surajood-deen Bahadur Shah Ghazee."

Despair began to reign in the rebels' hearts, and fanatic excitements were again resorted to. Hindoo pundits began to publish and sing wild and extravagant rhapsodies, of which the following may be a good specimen. After a portentous announcement, that he had arranged with the Almighty for preternatural agency, and had set the guards of Hanooman round the camp of the English, the rebel troops were thus addressed :—

> "No white-face can move out,
> Therefore advance your batteries without fear.
> The camp shall be destroyed like Lunka by fire;
> Increase the number of your guns.
> By the grace of Bulbhudder and Ramchunder
> The camp shall be annihilated.
> Fight without intermission day and night;
> Protect from injury our mother the cow.
> Offer sacrificial food to Joala Maee and Bhovanee,
> And distribute it among the Brahmins.
> Present daily an offering of fourteen cows.
> I have scrutinized the leaves of the book,
> Nirput Jee Jurria, and ascertain that Suneechur (the god of vengeance)
> Has descended upon the heads of the English.
> Offer sacrifices to Sunneechur;
> See what a moment will bring forth."

About the time when Heaven had been thus stormed with Brahminical supplication, a great *protége* of the King, and a bitter and fanatic enemy of the British, Hakeem Ahsanoollah Khan, had been cleverly outdiplomatized by Rujjub Ali, Meer Moonshee, under the guidance of the accomplished Hodson.

Rujjub Ali addressed his Mohamedan friend in a letter, couched in terms which, if the letter fell into the sepoys' hands, must infallibly lead them to infer the treachery of the Hakeem; and if not discovered by them the Hakeem's allegiance might be diverted to the British side. The letter was very clever, and the annexed couplet was introduced as probably applicable to the Hakeem's position, but certainly applicable to that of the puppet monarch. "A fly was seated on a piece of straw floating in the urine of an ass, and thought himself conducting a ship." Very shortly after the receipt of the letter, the Hakeem paid a visit to the Begum Sumroo's house, wherein was deposited the rebel powder manufactory. It exploded. This roused the suspicions of the sepoys, who rushed to the Hakeem's residence, searched it, and found the letter of Rujjub Ali; whereon they plundered the premises, gutted them completely, and finished by conflagration. The Hakeem narrowly escaped with life, by darting to the palace. Great divisions were the result of this adroit piece of tactics. A new powder manufactory, far out of the deadly range of British batteries, was erected at Dariogunge. The King's authority was spurned; he wished to abdicate. The enemy lost all unanimity, strength, and concert. Councils in the city, under different presidents, sat continually. Though with unity of action the annihilation of the British force, by simple overwhelming numbers, could hardly have been doubted, yet each new commander distrusted his rival. Fresh and heavy levies of money were made on the inhabitants, and a general and honest prayer for the return of peaceful times and British law and order was breathed around by the ruined trades people.

The mutineers felt that the disposition of their forces was accurately known. So soon as a damaging battery was erected from the interior, suggestions as to the position proper for another to silence it from the exterior, were tendered and carried out. Want of heart, the sure precursor of defeat, had began to be displayed. Bands which had remained with the mutinous brigades, assembled one evening before the tent of General Bukht Khan to celebrate fictitious captures and imaginary triumphs, and to shroud the ignominy of incessant defeats and almost daily loss of guns; but none were deceived by imposture so palpable. The King at last shut himself up: when he appeared in durbar he maintained a gloomy silence. The Mirza Mogul and General Bukht Khan were in open feud; which not even the contemplation of the certain ruin impending could contribute to appease, or yield to the cultivation of a good understanding. The latter complained that the former had demoralized his division, who were envious of the superior plunder obtained. The King attempted to harangue the army, declaring that "as he had never called them together, so they might disperse as soon as they liked." The Neemuch Brigade became particularly broken-spirited. The Bareilly Brigade showed symptoms of retirement. The steady monthly salaries under the British Government began to be missed; and the King had a third time to impose additional burdens on the wretched townspeople. But the golden egg had been extracted, and there were no supplies. Indications of partiality for the King's family were now (16th August) apparent even in the letters of correspondents. The names of Neill and Nicholson had become of terrific notoriety; and the most exaggerated reports of British reinforcements were again circulated and believed in. Upstart chieftains on all sides, and mushroom commanders, pestered the King of Delhi for subsidies and pecuniary aid. But the exchequer was empty.

The internal affairs of the city continued this wise until the 30th of August, when the correspondence to the camp became distinctly varied in its style, according as it was composed by a Mahomedan, or by a Hindoo. The approaching hour was known and feared. Of one, Heera Singh, who was made major of brigade of the Neemuch force, it is declared by a Hindoo correspondent that on the 13th of

August the King spoke to him "encouragingly," directed him to re-organize the brigade, and though he "could not give such guns as had been lost, he would replace them to the best of his ability."

Particular enumerations of the force which remained were made, for the information of the British camp; but these were only partially correct, both as to numbers and names. The 70th N. I., who were at Barrackpore, were named. There is mention of a leading character in the Gwalior Contingent who offered, if put in command of the whole force under the King's orders, to attack Agra; but the answer was to the effect that the King "could not interfere." The formidable nature of the Rohilkund insurrection was well known in Delhi; but the behaviour of the Nawab of Rampoor damped the ardour of the rebels; and the hill station at Nainee Tal has been preserved intact. From a Mahomedan correspondent we are informed of the enormous exertions which Muftee Sudder-ood-deen, the aforementioned Hukeem Ahsanoolah Khan, Mirza Ellahee Bux and Begum Zeenet Mahal are prepared to make for the English Government. Four thousand horsemen, irregulars, became suddenly possessed of an anxious desire to embrace their families once more if their lives were spared. The infantry were equally anxious for change of air. The zealous personages did not wish to screen "actual rebels, and would wish all those who had committed bloodshed and plunder to be severely punished" indeed; but the mercy of the Government is particularly asked for the "*King, the nobles, and the citizens of Delhi, who are innocent and helpless!*"

So distracted were the councils of the interior about the beginning of September, that frequently the British army was harassed by watching for premeditated night attacks, which never were made. The Neemuch Brigade on the 8th of September swore to conquer or die: Hindoo and Mussulman troops grasped hands and exchanged oaths not to desert.

More financial measures were resolved on. All villages near Boolundshuhur, which had befriended the British, were to be plundered for a fourth time; compulsory loans from the shopkeepers of the city were devised. The Mhow mutineers were reported to have crossed the Chumbul, and the city spies pressed that the grand assault should be made before their arrival. The population began to assume an ironical air in their responses to the king, and said "they were to go out to the attack, as they had enjoyed such quiet and happiness under the rule of the mutineers!" An emissary half-unnerved the whole city on the 9th of August, returning from the Punjab with a report that Sir John Lawrence, at the head of ten thousand men, had just arrived in camp to make a special attack.

About this period, also, the awful miseries of warfare, and the ghastly destitution of anarchy, were fully felt by the population, shop-keepers, and retail tradesmen; and as the day of retribution drew nigh, they began to seek, at the hands of the British army, that generous protection for their wives and for their children which in no instance had been extended to European maidenhood or infancy by their ferocious countrymen. Two thousand five hundred women and children tried to leave, and about six hundred carts blocked up the main streets; but all egress was prevented.

On the 9th of September, the rebel army became torn by intestine feuds; and the information of the spies became singularly precise as to the effect of the British fire, the positions of the rebel guns, and the measures adopted to resist the assault. Proclamations were issued that any Sikhs or Khakees who would desert from the British army and join the army of Islam, were to be received with open arms, and their devotion rewarded by jagheers.

According to the spies, about half of the Sikhs in

Delhi were inclined to the British side, but the other half fought even more determinedly against us; and it is possible that a considerable body deserted. All this information, however, had to be received, and was received, with due caution. Events proved the military details to be sufficiently reliable. Subsequently to this, and just previous to the assault, amidst the military details and general information, one picturesque incident breaks forth: that of the King—the last of the Moguls—appearing before his durbar, tearing his beard, snatching his turban from his hoary head, and invoking vengeance on those who had brought him to such an end by their cowardice and disunion. We must now return to the exterior of the city.

It has been mentioned that the position of the British army before Delhi was that of the besieged rather than of the besiegers. Even with the augmented force at his disposal, the General could not have completed the line of investment. The Chief Engineer, Lieutenant-Colonel Baird Smith, thus describes the characteristic features of the place:—"The eastern face of the city rests on the Jumna, and during the season of the year when our operations were carried on, the stream may be described as washing the base of the walls. All access to a besieger on the river front is, therefore, impracticable. The defences here consist of an irregular wall with occasional bastions and towers, and about one-half of the length of the river face is occupied by the palace of the King of Delhi, and its outwork, the old Mogul fort of Selimghur. The river may be described as the chord of a rough arc formed by the remaining defences at the place. These consist of a succession of bastioned fronts, the connection being very long, and the outworks limited to one crown-work at the Ajmere gate, and Martello towers mounting a single gun at such points as require some additional flanking fire to that given by the bastions themselves. The bastions are small, generally mounting three guns in each face, two in each flank, and one in embrasure at the salient. They are provided with masonry parapets about 12 feet in thickness, and have a relief of about 16 feet above the plane of site. The curtain consists of a simple masonry wall or rampart 16 feet in height, 11 feet thick at top, and 14 or 15 at bottom. This main wall carries a parapet loopholed for musketry 8 feet in height and 8 feet in thickness. The whole of the land front is covered by a beam of variable width ranging from 16 to 30 feet, and having a scarp wall 8 feet high. Exterior to this is a dry ditch, of about 25 feet in width, and from 16 to 20 feet in depth. The counterscarp is simply an earthen slope easy to descend. The glacis is a very short one extending only 50 or 60 yards from the counterscarp; using general terms, it covers from the besiegers' view from half to one-third of the height of the walls of the place. The defences, in a word, are 'modernized' forms of ancient works that existed when the city fell before Lord Lake's army in 1803. They extend about seven miles in circumference, and include an area of about three square miles. On the western side of Delhi there appear the last outlying spurs of the Aravelli Mountains, and represented here by a low ridge which disappears at its intersection with the Jumna, about two miles above the place. The drainage from the eastern slope of the ridge finds its way to the river along the northern and the north-western faces of the city, and has formed there a succession of parallels or connected ravines of considerable depth. By taking advantage of these hollow ways admirable cover was constantly obtained for the troops, and the labour of the siege was materially reduced. The whole of the exterior of the place presents an extraordinary mass of old buildings of all kinds—of thick brushwood and occasional clumps of forest trees, giving great facilities for cover, which, during the siege operations at least proved to be on the whole more favourable to us than to the enemy."

The most perfect success attended the plan of siege operations, and the noble Bengal Artillery has added another, if possible more lustrous, page to its long annals of glory and renown. Never was its fire more vigorous and effective. Associated with the recollection of the famous six days' open trenches before Delhi in 1857, will be handed down to posterity the reputation of the 9th Lancers and the 6th Dragoon Carabineers, who worked at the guns at each of the breaching batteries in common with their comrades of the Artillery. With no relief for the officers, and but little for the men, for seven and a half scorching days and nights, in the most sickly season of the year, did this gallant band keep up a galling fire. One breaching battery was entirely worked by men of the 9th Lancers, and aided by two sergeants of Artillery; a concentrated and vigorous fire was kept up on the walled space of the city included between the Water, the Moree, and the Cashmere Bastions.

Fifty-four siege guns were distributed to silence the enemy's fire, and four siege batteries were erected. The first, under Major Brind, completely ruined the defences of the Shah and Moree Bastions, while it protected the assaulting column from a flank fire, and diverted the fire of the enemy at the Cashmere Bastion from the working parties at the second battery. The first siege battery caught fire, and was destroyed on the 10th of September; but not before it had accomplished its task. Not until after the most urgent persuasions would Major Turner, who had joint command, be persuaded to leave the field, though sore stricken with sickness. The battery was not unmolested: night after night did the enemy in force come out and strive to destroy it.

The second siege battery, under Major Campbell, breached the curtain to the right of the Cashmere Bastion, dismounted nearly all the enemy's guns, stripped off the parapet, and thus left the mutineers without cover. The third siege battery, under Major Nott, which was armed on the night of the 11th instant, shelled the interior of the Water Bastion and the Church, pierced the wall on the 13th of September, and by the same evening had effected a practicable breach. The fourth siege battery, under Major Tombs, whom to mention is to praise, kept up, from the 14th of September, a ravaging fire on the Cashmere Gate, the Church, the Water Bastion, and Skinner's house.

On the night of the 13th September, Delhi became

ripe for assault; and hearts beat high when the bombardment ceased, and the order of the General commanding for the storm on the morning of the 14th was rapidly circulated through the camp.

The assault was delivered on four points. The first column was commanded by the lamented Brigadier-General Nicholson; who, to the grief of the army, sank under his wounds on the 20th of September. The second was led by Brigadier Jones, of the 60th Rifles; the third by Colonel Campbell, H. M.'s 52nd L. I.; the fourth by Major Reid. A reserve column was commanded by Brigadier Longfield. The despatches published will give the reader the exact results of the first momentous day.

But the devoted heroism of the Engineers, who formed the exploding party to blow away the Cashmere Gate, cannot be passed over. The deed was done, not stealthily, or by stratagem, nor under the broad black shield of night, but in open daylight. Lieutenants Salkeld and Home, of the Engineers, accompanied by a small band of heroes, Sergeant John Smith, A. B. Carmichael, Corporal Burgess, of the Sappers and Miners, Bugler Hawthorne, of H. M.'s 52nd, covered by the fire of the splendid 60th Rifles, were told off for the desperate and critical duty. Lieutenants Home, Smith, Carmichael, and Havildar Madho led with the powder bags.

Salkeld, with Corporal Burgess and the remainder, followed. On reaching the gateway, the advanced party found part of the drawbridge destroyed. Regardless of the precarious footing offered by the few remaining beams, the party pushed on nobly to lodge the powder at the gate. But the wicket was open, and a murderous fire issued from its portal. A sergeant fell dead after fixing the powder, and the havildar was wounded. But one-half of the perilous, though glorious, task was done. None dared to venture out to dislodge the bags, and the advanced party slipped down into the ditch, to permit of the advance of the firing party.

In attempting to fire, Lieutenant Salkeld fell fearfully wounded in two places; but while on the ground, he remembered England and his duty, and flung the slow match to Corporal Burgess, who had scarce appended the light to the train (in fact played the part on which, perhaps, the fate of British India depended), when he, too, fell mortally wounded. The noise of the explosion was a fitting salvo over the grave of such Englishmen. Bugler Hawthorne did his own dangerous work, and then repaired to the wounded Salkeld, bound up his wounds, and, careless of the hail of bullets, tenderly removed his dying commander.

We have thus led our readers up to the fall of Delhi. As the most appropriate close to this chapter, we republish the original despatches of General Wilson:—

From Major-General A. WILSON, *Commanding Delhi Field Force, to Captain* H. W. NORMAN, *Assistant Adjutant-General of the Army, Delhi.*

SIR, *Delhi,* 16*th September*, 1857.

I have the high satisfaction of reporting for the information of the Major-General commanding in the Upper Provinces, and through him of his Excellency the Commander-in-Chief, and of the Government, that on the morning of the 14th instant the force under my command assaulted the city of Delhi with success.

Under present circumstances, Major-General Gowan will, I trust, allow me to withhold for a time a full and complete detail of the operations from their commencement to their close, and to limit myself to a summary of events.

After six days of open trenches, during which the Artillery, and Engineers, under their respective commanding officers, Major Gaitskell and Lieutenant-Colonel Baird Smith, vied with each other in pushing on the works; two excellent and most practicable breaches were formed in the walls of the place, one in the curtain to the right of the Cashmere Bastion, the other to the left of the Water Bastion, the defences of those bastions and the parapets, giving musketry cover to the enemy commanding the breaches, having also been destroyed by the artillery.

The assault was delivered on four points. The first column, under Brigadier-General J. Nicholson, consisting of her Majesty's 75th Regiment (300 men), 1st European Bengal Fusiliers (200 men), and the 2nd Punjaub Infantry (450 men), assaulted the main breach, their advance being admirably covered by the 1st Battalion her Majesty's 60th Rifles, under Lieutenant-Colonel Jones. The operation was crowned with brilliant success; the enemy, after severe resistance, being driven from the Cashmere Bastion, the Main Guard, and its vicinity, in complete rout.

The 2nd Column, under Brigadier Jones, her Majesty's 60th Regiment, consisting of her Majesty's 8th Regiment (250 men), the 2nd European Bengal Fusiliers (250 men), and the 4th Regiment of Sikhs (350 men), similarly covered by the 60th Rifles, advanced on the Water Bastion, carried the breach, and drove the enemy from his guns and position with a determination and spirit which gave me the highest satisfaction.

The 3rd column, under Colonel Campbell, of Her Majesty's 52nd Light Infantry, consisting of his own regiment (200 men), the Kumaon Battalion (250 men), and the 1st Punjaub Infantry (500 men), was directed against the Cashmere gateway. This column was preceded by an explosion party under Lieutenants Home and Salkeld, of the Engineers, covered by the 60th Rifles. The demolition of the gate having been accomplished, the column forced an entrance, overcoming a strenuous opposition from the enemy's infantry and heavy artillery, which had been brought to bear on the position. I cannot express too warmly my admiration of the gallantry of all concerned in this difficult operation.

The reserve, under Brigadier Longfield, her Majesty's 8th Regiment, composed of her Majesty's 61st Regiment (250 men), 4th Punjaub Rifles, (450 men), the Belooch Battalion (300 men), the Jheend Rajah's Auxiliaries (300 men), and 200 of her Majesty's 60th Rifles, who joined after the assault had been made, awaited the result of the attack, and on the columns entering the place, took possession of the post I had previously assigned to it. This duty was ultimately performed to my entire satisfaction.

The firm establishment of the reserve rendering the assaulting columns free to act in advance, Brigadier - General Nicholson, supported by Brigadier Jones, swept the ramparts of the place from the Cashmere to the Cabul gate, occupying the bastions and defences, capturing the guns, and driving the enemy before him. During the advance, Brigadier-General Nicholson was, to the grief of myself and the whole army, dangerously wounded; the command consequently devolved on Brigadier Jones, who, finding the enemy in great force, occupying, and pouring a destructive fire from the roofs of strong and commanding houses in the city on all sides, the ramparts themselves being enfiladed by guns, prudently resolved on retaining possession of the Cabul gate, which his troops had so gallantly won, in which he firmly established himself, awaiting the result of the operations of the other columns of occupation.

Colonel Campbell with the column under his command advanced successfully from the Cashmere-gate by one of the main streets beyond the Chandnee Chouk, the central and principal street of the city, towards the Jumma Musjid, with the intention of occupying that important post. The opposition, however, which he met from the great concentration of the enemy at the Jumma Musjid and the houses in the neighbourhood, he himself, I regret to state being wounded, satisfied him that his most prudent course was not to maintain so advanced a position with the comparatively limited force at his disposal, and he accordingly withdrew the head of his column, and placed himself in communication with the reserve, a measure which had my entire approval, I having previously determined that in the event of serious opposition being encountered in the town itself, it would be most inexpedient to commit my small force to a succession of street fights, in which their gallantry, discipline, and organization could avail them so little.

My present position, therefore, is that which, under such a contingency, I had resolved to occupy and establish myself in firmly, as the base of my systematic operations for the complete possession of the city. This embraces the magazine on one side, and the Cabul gate on the other, with the Moree, Cashmere, and Water Bastions, and strong intermediate posts, with secure communication along the front and to the rear.

From this base I am now cautiously pressing the enemy on all points with a view to establishing myself in a second advanced position, and I trust before many days to have it in my power to announce to the Supreme Government that the enemy have been driven from their last stronghold in the palace, fort, and streets of Delhi.

Simultaneously with the operations above detailed, an attack was made on the enemy's strong position outside the city in the suburbs of Kishengunge and Pahareepore, with a view of driving in the rebels, and supporting the main attack by effecting an entrance at the Cabul gate after it should be taken.

The force employed in this difficult duty I entrusted to that admirable officer, Major C. Reid, commanding the Sirmoor Battalion, whose distinguished conduct I have already had occasion prominently to bring to the notice of superior authority, and who was, I regret deeply to state, severely wounded on this occasion. The column consisted of his own battalion, detachments of the Rifles, 1st Fusiliers, the Guides, and other regiments, amounting in all to about 1,000 men, supported by the auxiliary troops of his Highness the Maharajah Rumbeer Singh under Captain R. Lawrence.

The strength of the positions, however, and the desperate resistance offered by the enemy, withstood for a time the effort of the troops, gallant though they were, and the combination was unable to be effected. The delay, I am happy to say, has been only temporary, for the enemy have subsequently abandoned their position, leaving their guns in our hands.

In this attack I found it necessary to support Major Reid with Cavalry and Horse Artillery, both of which arms were admirably handled respectively by Brigadier Grant, of Her Majesty's 9th Lancers, Commanding the Cavalry Brigade, and Major H. Tombs, of the Horse Artillery, who inflicted severe punishment on the enemy, though I regret their own loss was very heavy.

The resistance of the rebels up to this time has been that of desperate men, to which must be attributed the severe loss we have sustained, amounting proximately, so far as I am able to judge in the absence of returns of casualties, to 46 officers killed and wounded, and about 800 men. Amongst those whose services the State has been deprived of, are many officers of distinction and merit, holding superior commands, and whose places cannot be supplied; and I have specially to lament that I have been deprived of the services of no less than nine officers of that splendid corps, the Engineers, one of whom was killed, and others seriously wounded in the gallant performance of their duty.

Until I receive reports from Brigadiers and other commanding officers, I am unable to enter more fully into the details of these operations, and I trust the circumstances under which I write will excuse any slight inaccuracies or imperfections which my despatch may exhibit.

The absence of such reports also prevents my bringing to notice the names of those officers and men who have specially distinguished themselves. This will be my grateful duty hereafter. But I cannot defer the expression of my admiration for the intrepidity, coolness and determination of all engaged—officers and men, Europeans and natives of all arms.

I have, &c.,
(Signed) A. Wilson, *Major-General,*
Commanding Delhi Field Force.

From Major-General A. Wilson, *Commanding Delhi Field Force, to the Adjutant-General of the Army, Delhi.*

Dated Delhi, 22nd September, 1857.

Sir,

In continuation of my despach of the 16th instant, I now have the honour to forward a report, for the information the Major-General Commanding in the Upper Provinces, His Excellency the Commander-in-Chief, and the Government, of the further operations of the force under my command since that date.

During the 17th and 18th we continued to take up advanced posts in the face of considerable opposition on the part of the rebels, and not without loss to ourselves—two officers being killed, and a number of men killed and wounded. On the evening of the 19th the Burn Bastion, which had given us considerable annoyance, was surprised and captured. On the morning of the 20th our troops pushed on and occupied the Lahore gate, from which an unopposed advance was made on the other bastions and gateways until the whole defences were in our hands.

From the time of our first entering the city an uninterrupted and vigorous fire from our guns and mortars was kept up on the palace, Jumma Musjid, and other important posts in possession of the rebels, and as we took up our various positions in advance, our light guns and mortars were brought forward and used with effect on the streets and houses in their neighbourhood.

The result of this heavy and unceasing bombardment, and of the steady and persevering advance of our troops, has been the evacuation of the palace by the King, entire desertion of the city by the inhabitants, and the precipitate flight of the rebel troops, who abandoning their camp property, many of their sick and wounded, and the greater part of their field artillery, have fled in utter disorganization; some 4,000 or 5,000 across the bridge-of-boats into the Doab, the remainder along the right bank of the Jumna.

The gates of the palace having been blown in, it was occupied by our troops at about noon on the 20th, and my Head-Quarters established in it on the same day.

The great diminution of our strength by losses in action during the last few days, added to the severe sickness prevailing among the troops, has prevented my immediately organizing and sending a column in pursuit, but a force,* under Command of Lieutenant-Colonel Greathed, will march to-morrow morning towards Boolundshuhur and Allyghur to intercept the rebels, whose intentions are said to be to cross the Jumna. My intelligence, however, I regret to say, is very defective.

The King, who accompanied the troops, it is believed, for some short distance last night, gave himself up to a party of Irregular Cavalry, whom I had sent out in the direction of the fugitives, and he is now a prisoner under a guard of European soldiers. Three of the Shahzadas,† who are known to have taken a prominent part in the atrocities attending the insurrec-

* 1st Troop 1st Brigade Horse Artillery, 3rd Troop 1st Brigade 3rd Horse Artillery, No. 17 Light Field Battery, two Companies Punjab Sappers, 9th Lancers, 1st, 2nd, and 5th Punjab Cavalry, Hodson's Horse (200), H.M.'s 8th Regiment, H.M.'s 75th Regiment, 2nd and 4th Punjab Infantry.

† Mirza Mogul, Mirza Khoje Sultan, sons of the King, and Mirza Aboo Bukker, grandson.

tion, have been this day captured by Captain Hodson, and shot on the spot.

Thus has the important duty committed to this force been accomplished, and its object attained. Delhi, the focus of rebellion and insurrection, and the scene of so much horrible cruelty, taken and made desolate—the King a prisoner in our hands, and the mutineers, notwithstanding their great numerical superiority, and their vast resources in ordnance and all the munitions and appliances of war, defeated on every occasion of engagement with our troops, are now driven with slaughter in confusion and dismay from their boasted stronghold.

The details of the operation have been so fully entered into in my previous despatch, and in the annexed reports and returns from the various commanding officers, that little remains for me to say—but to again express my unqualified approbation of the conduct and spirit of the whole of the troops—not only on this occasion but during the entire period they have been in the field.

For four months of the most trying season of the year this force, originally very weak in number, has been exposed to the repeated and determined attacks of an enemy far out-numbering it, and supported by a numerous and powerful artillery. The duties imposed upon all have been laborious, harassing, and incessant; and, notwithstanding heavy losses both in action and from disease, have been at all times zealously and cheerfully performed.

I beg to add my most cordial concurrence in the commendations bestowed by officers commanding brigades, columns and detachments on the officers and men named in their several reports; and I have to express my own deep obligations to those officers themselves for the valuable assistance I have at all times received from them.

To Major F. Gaitskell, who recently assumed command of the artillery in the field, consequent on Brigadier Garbett having been disabled by a wound, and to the officers and men of that distinguished arm, to whose energy and untiring zeal the successful issue of the operations is so largely attributable, I have to offer my hearty thanks; and particularly am I indebted to that excellent officer, Lieut.-Colonel C. Hogge, Director of the Artillery Depôt, who volunteered his services as commissary of ordnance with the siege train, through whose able superintendence of the park and arrangements for the supply of ammunition to the batteries, our artillery was able to deal out the destruction which was effected; as also to Capt. T. Young, Deputy-Commissary, and Mr. J. Stotesbury, Assistant-Commissary of Ordnance, for their exertions during the whole siege.

To Lieut.-Colonel Baird Smith, Chief Engineer, who in ill health, and whilst suffering from the effects of a painful wound, devoted himself with the greatest ability and assiduity to the conduct of the difficult and important operations of the siege, to his gallant and eminently talented second, Captain A. Taylor, and to the whole of the officers and men of the Engineer Brigade, my thanks and acknowledgments are especially due for having planned and successfully carried out in the face of extreme and unusual difficulties an attack almost without parallel in the annals of siege operations.

To that most brilliant officer, Brigadier-General J. Nicholson, whose professional character and qualifications are so well known and appreciated, I am under the greatest obligations for the daring manner in which he led his column to the assault; and I deeply deplore that his services are for the present lost to the State.

To Brigadier Hope Grant, C.B., commanding the Cavalry Brigade, and to Brigadiers J. Longfield and W. Jones, C.B., commanding Infantry Brigades, I am deeply indebted. And I have to offer my best thanks to Colonel C. Campbell, commanding Her Majesty's 52nd Light Infantry, and to that intrepid and excellent officer, Major C. Reid, of the Sirmoor Battalion, both wounded whilst gallantly leading columns of attack; as also to Colonel J. Jones, commanding the 1st Battalion 60th Royal Rifles, a regiment which has shown a glorious example both in its daring gallantry and its perfect discipline to the whole force, for the ability with which he covered the advance of the assaulting columns.

I have pleasure also in bringing favourably to notice the

services rendered by Lieut.-Colonel H. P. Burn, attached as field officer to the 1st Brigade of Infantry, and by Captain Seymour Blane, Her Majesty's 52nd Light Infantry, Major of Brigade to Brigadier-General Nicholson.

Colonel J. L. Denniss, of Her Majesty's 52nd Light Infantry, whom I placed in charge of the camp during the operations, is entitled to my thanks and acknowledgments for the able disposition he made with the troops under his command for the due protection of his important charge.

To the officers of the general staff of the army, and to those of the staff of the field force, my cordial acknowledgments are due for the admirable manner in which they have performed their responsible duties; to that very distinguished officer, Brigadier General W. Chamberlain, Adjutant-General of the Army, who, though still incapacitated by a severe wound previously received, proceeded to the ridge at Hindoo Rao's, and performed essential service after Major Reid had been wounded, and it became necessary to resume that position to Captain H. M. Norman, Assistant Adjutant-General of the Army, who on this, as on each and every occasion, has been distinguished by his gallantry, zeal, and professional ability; to that experienced officer, Major R. S. Ewart, Deputy Assistant Adjutant-General, and his gallant and energetic coadjutor Captain D. M. Stewart, Deputy Assistant Adjutant-General, who have conducted the duties of their important department with the force, much to my satisfaction; and to Captain E. B. Johnson, Assistant Adjutant-General of Artillery, who volunteered to command the 24-pounder Breaching Battery, most ably and effectually carried out the duty assigned to him, and who rejoined my personal staff on the morning of the assault, and who has throughout these operations given me the most zealous and efficient support; I am greatly indebted for the assistance they have afforded me.

I also beg to bring very favourably to notice the officers of the Quartermaster-General's Department, Captain D. C. Chute and Captain H. M. Garstin, and Captain W. S. R. Hodson, who has performed such good and gallant service with his newly-raised regiment of Irregular Horse, and at the same time conducted the duties of the intelligence department under the orders of the Quartermaster-General with rare ability and success: also that active and gallant officer, Lieutenant F. S. Roberts, attached to the Artillery Brigade in the capacity of Deputy Assistant Quartermaster-General.

Lieutenant-Colonel Keith Young, Judge Advocate General, also, and his Deputies, Captain F. C. Maisey, and Captain H. W. Wilson, most zealously assisted me in carrying my orders.

To the officers of my personal staff, Captain C. H. Barchard, who has served with me first as my orderly officer, and subsequently as Aide-de-Camp, and to whose zealous and untiring exertions I am deeply indebted; to Captain J. R. Turnbull, Second Aide-de-Camp, Captain R. A. Lowe and Lieutenant R. C. Lowe, Extra Aide-de-Camp, I am under great obligations for the zeal and readiness with which they on this and all other occasions have performed their duties. My thanks are also due to Major H. A. Ouvry, who attended me on the day of assault.

For the valuable aid at all times rendered by officers of the Civil Service, who have been attached to the force, I have to record my warm acknowledgments; to Mr. Hervey Greathed, Agent to the Lieutenant-Governor North-West Provinces (whose subsequent sudden death I deeply lament), and Mr. C. B. Saunders, both of whom attended me in action, and made themselves most useful; Sir T. Metcalfe, Bart., whose gallantry in conducting Colonel Campbell's assaulting column through the city was conspicuous; and Mr. R. W. Clifford, who was also in attendance on me, are all entitled to my thanks.

Whilst, however, in acknowledging the services of those officers whose good fortune it was to be present at the assault and in the action of the 14th, I have only performed a grateful duty. I should be greatly wanting if I failed to record the names of those who have previously distinguished themselves, but who, incapacitated by wounds or sickness, were unable to join in the operations of that day. Amongst these I have specially to notice Brigadier St. G. D. Showers, whose cool gallantry on the numerous occasions in which he has been engaged has been conspicuous; also Colonel A. W. M. Becher, Quartermaster-General of the Army, who, though prevented by a severe wound received in June last from taking an active part in the field, has at all times rendered me zealous assistance. Lieutenant-Colonel T. Seaton, C.B., of the 35th Native Infantry, attached to the force, a most valuable and experienced officer, of whose services I have been deprived owing to a wound received by him on the 23rd July; that admirable officer, Lieutenant-Colonel Murray Mackenzie, commanding the 1st Brigade of Horse Artillery, of whose services I have also been deprived by a wound which he received when in charge of the heavy batteries at an early stage of our operations; that officer so distinguished in our frontier warfare, Major J. Coke, commanding the 1st Punjab Rifles, severely wounded at the head of his regiment on the 12th August; and the gallant commander of the Guides, Captain H. D. Daly, who was very severely wounded leading a most daring charge on the enemy's guns in the action of the 19th June.

I need not observe how largely the success and efficiency of the army depends on the regularity of its supplies. Under circumstances of peculiar difficulty, in a district the population of which has been inimical, and in which civil authority has ceased to exist, this force has from the commencement been kept well and sufficiently provisioned with supplies of every description, the issue of rations to the soldier having been as regular, both in quantity and quality, as in cantonments. My warmest thanks are, therefore, due to Lieutenant-Colonel W. B. Thompson, Deputy-Commissary-General, the admirable and indefatigable head of that department in the field; as also to Lieutenant T. H. Sibley, Principal Executive Officer; to Lieutenant Waterfield, and to the other officers serving in that department.

With the medical arrangements of Superintending-Surgeon E. Tritton I have every reason to be satisfied, and he is entitled to my cordial acknowledgments. At such a trying season of the year, and in a notoriously unhealthy locality, the sickness and mortality have of course been heavy. In addition to those suffering from disease, the hospitals have received almost daily accessions of wounded men. The labours, therefore, of the medical department have been unceasing. Notwithstanding there has not been at any time the slightest failure in the arrangements for the care and comfort of the very numerous patients.

Amongst those medical officers whose unwearied zeal and superior ability have come prominently before me are Officiating Superintending Surgeon C. McKinnon, M.D., who has been in medical charge of the 1st Brigade Horse Artillery; Surgeon J. H. Ker Innes, 60th Royal Rifles; Surgeon E. Hare, of the 2nd Fusiliers; Assistant-Surgeon J. J. Clifford, M.D., of the 9th Lancers; and Assistant-Surgeon W. F. Mactier, M.D., on the personal staff of the late Commander-in-Chief.

Credit is also due to Assistant-Surgeon D. Scott, M.D., Medical Storekeeper.

The duties and offices of Provost Marshal to the force have been conducted by a very deserving old non-commissioned officer, Sergeant-Major Stroud, 3rd Brigade Horse Artillery, whom I recommend to favourable consideration for a commission. The names of other non-commissioned officers, deserving of a similar reward, I shall have the pleasure of submitting hereafter.

I should neither be fulfilling the repeatedly-expressed wishes of the artillery officers attached to this force, nor following the dictates of my own inclination, if I failed to acknowledge the valuable assistance which has throughout the operations before Delhi been most cheerfully given by the non-commissioned officers and men of Her Majesty's 9th Lancers and the 6th Dragoon Guards in working the batteries; without it, owing to the comparatively small number of artillerymen, I should have been quite unable to man the batteries efficiently, or keep up the heavy fire which, aided by these men, I have happily been able to do. To these regiments, therefore, and to Brigadier Grant, who so readily placed a certain number of his men at my disposal for such purpose, I tender my best thanks.

It would be an omission on my part were I to pass over in silence the good services and loyal conduct of one who has already been rewarded by the Government for the friendly assistance he rendered to our army in Affghanistan—I allude to Nawab Jan Fishan Khan, who, with his brave nephew, Sirdar Bahadoor Meer Khan, and their retainers, accompanied me from Meerut, was present at the actions on the Hindun, and has since taken part in nearly every action in which this force has been engaged.

Of the loyal services rendered to the State by the Rajah of Putteeala, which must be so well known to the Government, it may not be considered necessary for me to speak; but it is incumbent on me, in my capacity as Commander of this force, to acknowledge officially the great assistance the Rajah's troops have afforded me in enabling the numerous convoys of ammunition and stores to travel in security and safety to my camp under their escort and protection.

It is my duty to bring prominently to the notice of Government the admirable service performed by the Jheend Rajah and his troops, under command of Lieutenant-Colonel H. F. Dunsford; they have not only had very harassing duties to carry out in the constant escort of convoys of sick and wounded men, ammunition, &c., but they have also aided me in the field on more than one occasion, and finally participated in the assault of the city.

Lastly, I trust I may be excused if I thus publicly acknowledge the all-important and valuable aid for which I am indebted to the Chief Commissioner of the Punjab, Sir John Lawrence, K.C.B., to whose indefatigable exertions, in reinforcing me with every available soldier in the Punjab, the successful result of our operations is, I unhesitatingly pronounce, attributable; and I take this opportunity of recognising the advantage derived from the presence of the troops of his Highness the Maharajah Runbeer Singh, in alliance with the British force, the moral effect of which has been great; and although unsuccessful, I regret to say, in the actual accomplishment of that part of the operations in which the Jummoo Contingent was engaged on the 14th, I can attach no particle of blame to those troops, as I consider, under the circumstances in which they were placed, the very strong position which they had to attack, and the prolonged and determined resistance which they encountered from an enemy superior to them in number, arms, training, and experience, that they behaved under their gallant commander, Captain R. Lawrence, and the other British officers serving with them, to whom my best thanks are due, as well as they could have been expected to do.

Captain Lawrence's report of his operations is annexed.

I have, &c.,

(Signed) A. WILSON, *Major-General,*
Commanding Delhi Field Force.

CHAPTER IX.

CONCLUDING REMARKS.

It is to be feared that many excellent actions, much private heroism, and moral as well as physical chivalry, have, from necessarily contracted private sources of information, escaped merited notice: to such incidents history will do justice; but if any palpable omission has been made, the compiler offers his apologies to those aggrieved.

The Punjab Government make no pretensions to infallibility in their counsels or finality in their administrative machine; much less would it claim credit for prophetic political foresight, because of the extraordinary fidelity, loyalty, and even attachment, shown to their rulers generally by the Punjab people in the past perilous conjuncture. Still whatever credit is due for the success attending the determined pursuit of an original and bold line of policy, is fairly theirs. The impression of inherent invincibility was kept up; and the ignorance of the Asiatic as to the universality and overwhelming nature of the danger was boldly counted on. The announcement of the speedy arrival of vast reinforcements from England was as calmly made, as if the proverbial apathy of the British Parliament was to be roused from its sleep of a hundred years on Indian subjects by a single summons, however black the tidings. The full force of the danger, and the form in which it would approach, were to them matters of conjecture, but anxiously and justly enough appreciated by Indians. To have ever acted on the defensive—ever, much less then—would have ruined our prestige, and only staved off the evil day for the Punjab for a few short weeks. Further, without securing certain tranquillity it would have lost us the important political advantage of using the hereditary and inextinguishable aversion of the Sikhs to the Poorbeah, as the strongest and most malevolent weapon in the fight. The outbreak had been precipitated by about ten days; and in those days every golden moment was used.

The reader has seen what the decision and nerve of a Montgomery accomplished at Lahore; how his example was followed at Peshawur; what Sir John Lawrence has done finally for the resumption of empire in Hindoostan; and what the Punjab could have done for it (but for the first decisive step of the

13th May), with forty thousand Poorbeah soldiers in simultaneous revolt.

It was a rough awakening, but a complete one. The universality of the design was obvious. The Queen's Regiments on the 24th of May fired a "feu de joie" with blank ammunition on parade, and the unsuspecting Europeans were to have been massacred before reaching their lines. The sepoys at Fort William, Allahabad, Lahore, Govindgurh, Phillour, were to have seized those strongholds, while the green flag was hoisted at Delhi and the empire of Bahadoor Shah proclaimed. He was, it is believed, to have been endowed with the empire of his ancestors; the licentious Nawab of Moorshedabad was to have assumed the vice-royalty of Oudh; and to the protection of the ex-King of Oudh was to have been confided the care of Bahar and Bengal, while he assumed the purple, superseding the Governor-General of India.

Rapidly surveying the aspect of affairs, Sir John Lawrence at once foresaw the necessity of providing additional force for the Punjab: he predicted to the Governor-General, in a telegram of the 12th of May, the certainty that the greater portion of the native regular army would have to be disarmed! The Governor-General promptly accorded full plenipotentiary powers to the Chief Commissioner. The latter forthwith stopped all private leave; recalled all officers from Cashmere; directed the concentration of Europeans at all important places; and deprecating the error of detaching small bodies in various directions, commenced the raising of one thousand Mooltanee horse. He acquiesced in the valuable suggestion of Colonel Edwardes of calling in the hill tribes; ordered all mounted police into station head-quarters; calmly and courteously thanked, and directed such thanks to be offered, to the petty Sikh Chiefs who had at once pressed forward with offers of aid; and after these preliminary steps, sternly and manfully set himself to the stupendous task which, from the terrible delays in the original march of the army of Delhi, he felt convinced was in store for him.

The Chief Commissioner had already earnestly suggested the recall of the Persian troops, and the interception of the Chinese expedition; using the expression that every available European was necessary to *save the country!* He had empowered Colonel Edwardes to carry out the extreme sentence of the law; had ordered the director of public instruction (while leaving the English press entirely unfettered) to prepare sedative articles for the native journals, to allay public excitement; he had issued the most minute and varied orders on all sides for the provision of transport, and on the regulation of caste and sects, which should compose the new levies; orders containing suggestions replete with wisdom and the maturest insight into the Asiatic element. He had declined to permit any native chieftain to raise troops for us; at the same time accepting their aid for the district officers.

Such is a brief outline of the preliminary steps. A foremost one, however, was to secure the cordial allegiance of the chieftains in the most dangerous proximity. The Dost was subsidized into quiescence; Goolab Singh was cajoled into active allegiance; the Nawab of Bahawulpore was intimidated into neutrality; the Maharajah of Putiala required no summons: he was already in the field. His aid secured, or rather his "rôle" in the drama, confirmed the attitude of every other wavering chieftain. The Jheend Rajah outrivalled even the Putiala chief by the activity of his movements. The news from home showed that the crisis had been either under estimated or weakly palliated; whereas every day became more menacing. The Government nerved itself in the Punjab to greater and greater efforts, and reinforcements poured down to the fast thinning ranks before Delhi.

All semblance of Government in the North-West Provinces was nearly at an end. The exaggerated elaboration of its routine, and ramification of its legal defences—distasteful to those who had to administer it, and incomprehensible to the people—furnished no hope that any district could be held by moral force, founded either upon its merits, or upon affectionate reminiscences of its modes of procedure. In Mozaffernugger and other districts the first thing the populace did was to burn all the records. Devout aspirations were breathed, even by high authority, that in the Agra conflagrations might be included all the criminal and civil records. Thus district after district, though not occupied by a single mutineer, after a stagger broke up. The scattered and isolated instances of individual devotion and official loyalty, only showed in a more appalling light the total want of real sympathy, the time-serving policy of the revenue-paying masses, and the alienation of the half-educated population.

In some of the oldest conquered provinces, the popular resentment—on the natural principle of liberty implanted in man against usurpation, and the popular contempt of the real power of the usurper—has been most marked. In the North-West Provinces the civil establishments suffered nearly instantaneous collapse; and yet in almost every district, as it is recovered and submits to sway, every individual in official employ will be realizable, with dread secrets and unctuous stories in his heart; but not a fact to show as a set-off to the million plausible excuses for his absence when danger was near. Centralization exists together with divided responsibility, and the result is neutralization of force and waste of power. The Judge moved in the same social circle, but breathed a different popular and official atmosphere to that of the collector; and their "sets" revolved in separate systems. The fortunate absence of a superior officer enabled a Spankie at Saharanpore to hold his own in the teeth of unsurpassed difficulties, Goojur villages rampant, and Rohilkund in insurrection; and at Mirzapore a Tucker again maintained the reputation of the family. There may be others, but how few!

Under the Punjab system there is a recognized responsible head to each district, who originates, harmonizes, adopts, and acts. He is the authorized exponent of the political position of the Government, as well of its laws and institutions. Hence he is the referee in the first instance in every matter, domestic, social, or public. He enjoys, in common with the commandants of the Irregular Corps (which have generally proved successful experiments), the reality, as well as the responsibility of power. All his vigilance, tact, influence, if he possesses such essentials, could be used to good purpose in the crisis, and without fear of neutralization. He could appease excited feelings, allay curiosity; and conversing, as he has to do daily, with native gentlemen and chieftains keenly alive to the state of affairs, could execrate in common with them the horrors inflicted on miserable surviving women and little children. He could awake common sympathy. He could point out and elicit acquiescence in sentiment in regard to the speciality of the crisis; the degeneracy from high Asiatic honour of the Poorbeah Asiatic. He could glory with them in the story of the grand old faqueer who brought a European child in his arms to European protection at the risk of his own life, himself bleeding from wounds, and who would take no reward. He could fairly point out the manifest opportunity now offered to the unemployed mass of society in the Punjab, of congenial and honourable service, and lay before them the advantages and the reward; of which the degenerate Hindoostanees had shown themselves so grossly unworthy. Honesty saved the policy. The results of disloyalty were calmly and prophetically discussed—certain anarchy; disorder; domestic misery; riot; uncertainty.

For ten years, a practical commentary on the difference between the Anglo-Saxon and the Sikh dynasties had been presented to the understanding of every chieftain, every landowner, every trader, every capitalist, in the Punjab. The different uses to which conquests and temporary elevations to supreme power can be put, commended itself to the appreciation of each. The fostering care of Lord Dalhousie had not been lavished in vain.

The name of "Lawrence" alone represented power. Associated in the affectionate recollections of the people with the chivalrous gallantry, the cultivated understanding, the urbane demeanour, and princely munificence of the great Sir Henry, was their respect for the strong sagacity and the rough will, though scarcely less kind heart, of Sir John Lawrence. The two never dissociated from one single sphere of action, the amalgamation of the law into a name, "Lawrence," formed the ideal of a governing impersonation. What the Punjab lost in Sir Henry, it seemed at once to have gained in the calm and impassible, though resolute and high-souled Mr. Montgomery.

Thus, the country of our latest, and fiercest, and most chivalrous foe, through being preserved and used more in accordance with the genius and capacity of its people, has maintained an attitude unrivalled throughout the length and breadth of the troubled land. The fact is not stated as a matter for exultation, but for humble and hopeful thankfulness that some plan has been at last hit upon, and worked out with persevering sagacity and singleness of purpose, whereby the European can touch the native heart, and his mind's thoughts become intelligible; and some development of actual sympathy between the government and the governed be, however slightly, attained. Truly God Almighty with his own right hand and stretched out arm has gotten himself the victory. The loyalty of the Punjab once assured, every subsequent mutiny in the territories were absolutely Divine blessings: they relieved the Government of the task of the charge of suspected men, and rendered it free to send more and more troops to the great centre of action.

Of the Punjab Government it may indeed be said, "Alone they did it." It created an army of twenty-eight thousand men; of which there were, in round figures, thirteen thousand regular troops, seven thousand mounted levies, and nine thousand foot levies. With the exception of H. M.'s 60th Rifles, the Carabineers, and artillery originally drawn from Meerut, the whole of the Delhi field force was from the Punjab. Not a single native regiment was forthcoming from below. During the four chequered and momentous months preceding the capture of Delhi, was it all peace at home in the Punjab? The foregoing pages will have been written in vain, if the reader has not seen that there were murders, mutinies, incendiarisms, conspiracies, disloyalty, disarmings, battles, executions, pursuits, panics, and treacheries, sufficient to tax the utmost energies for the preservation of internal peace alone; setting aside the glorious and immortal task which the Punjab Government at once accepted, of saving the British empire in the East.

The first tidings from Delhi sent a spasm to the heart of every Christian in the Punjab. The tidings of the instantaneous disarming at Meean Meer sounded the réveille to every Englishman. The commonest European soldier seemed to attain an unwonted moral elevation of character. Like *Cœur-de-Lion* in the lists of Ashby-de-la-Zouche, the Anglo-Saxon seemed to have emulated the "*noir faineant*" and slept in his saddle. Such was the enormous vital energy, moral as well as physical, evoked. The natives believe it to consist in the truth of the significant saying that every European in India fights in his shroud. Let us look higher, and hope that the Anglo-Saxon race, like Cromwell's Ironsides, can not only fight for their country, but pray also to the God of Battles. The attributes and instincts of one quarter of the human species were pitted against another quarter. The Asiatic mind laid siege to the Anglo-Saxon mind on his own chosen vantage ground. The want or the presence of an extra European regiment has everywhere decided the physical contest. Unfathomable in design, unmatched in chicane, transcendant in powers of secret communion, bit by bit, inch by inch, had the Asiatic laid the great mine. Everything was diplomatically perfect: nothing was wanting but success. When the day dawned for the bold open field of thought and action, all ended in barbarous and ignominious failure — like the flight of the brilliant but unstable hordes of Darius before the Macedonian Phalanx.

At Allahabad the famous fort could not be wrested from a handful of stout old British pensioners. The illustrious defence of Jellalabad has paled before the spectacle of a British regiment holding out, for six months, at Lucknow, in the midst of a hostile population of ten millions, in the heart of the vilest capital in the world filled by more than two hundred thousand armed enemies; and assailed by the whole of the mutinous Oude forces, augmented by the rabble of the provincial chieftains.

Thus, as the days of temporization, of moral

influence, of conciliation and diplomacy swept hurriedly by, and the great plot was bared, the amazed and baffled sepoy discovered the power of the nation which can conquer though beleaguered. Again it will be said in Europe, "The British do not know when they are beaten." The idea of retreat, even with the lustre of a Xenophon, scarcely entered one bosom. According to rule, for a handful of Europeans to make head against the rebellion of an empire, outnumbering them by millions to their fifties, was fatuity, and they ought decently to have succumbed to their inevitable fates. The continent of Europe during the great struggle might have been looking on with ill-dissembled glee at Great Britain's fancied extremity; whereas the harbinger of her greatest triumph has already heralded the downfall of the seat of Islamism in India. To those fond of reading signs, we would point to the solitary golden cross still gleaming aloft on the summit of the Christian church in Delhi, whole and untouched; though the ball on which it rests is riddled with shots deliberately fired by the infidel populace. The cross symbolically triumphant over a shattered globe!

APPENDICES.

APPENDIX A.

Translation of a Letter from Moulvee Rujjub Ali Khan, to Hakeem Ahsanoollah Khan.

30th July, 1857.

I give you a piece of advice, do not make any excuses, but hear it.

Whatever a kind instructor says to you receive it.

Hakeem Sahib, wise as Plato, philosophic as Aristotle, unrivalled in wisdom in this age, Hakeem Ahsanoollah Khan, peace be to you.

Having laid aside the usual ceremonies I come to the subject matter of this letter which is as follows :—About two months have elapsed that the troops who ate the salt of the English Government, not keeping in view the ill consequences at the end, came to Delhi, and having raised the dust of tumult and disturbance, got a bad name to his Majesty the King of Delhi, and having stepped out of their proper sphere, have stood up as competitors of the English Government of supreme dignity.

The state of these rebel troops is just as described in the following verse of Mowlana Room :—

" A blade of grass in the urine of an ass was floating;
A fly having sat upon it, thought herself a ship conducting."

To the enlightened minds of his Majesty, of yourself, and to those of the wise men of the seven kingdoms (*i. e.* of the whole globe) the supremacy and power of the English Government is well-known. The fact of the English Government having assisted the Sultan of Turkey with troops, both in sea and land, and of having protected the Mahomedan empire against Russia at the expense of their own men and money, notwithstanding the English and European nations professed the same religion (*i. e.* Christianity) are so conspicuous as the light of the meridian sun. This is also known to all that from the commencement of the British rule in India the English rulers have never used force or authority in making the Hindoos and Mahomedans to learn the doctrines of Christianity, but that from the beginning to the present day the people of India are left in perfect liberty to live in peace, and to do as they think proper for bettering their condition in this world, and in that which is to come. The numberless benefits which the English Government have imparted to the people of India, and which entitle the English to gratitude and love from our part, are well impressed in your enlightened mind, and, therefore, it is quite unnecessary to enlarge this letter by an enumeration of them. From the history of Ferishta it appears that Abul Futah Jallalloodeen Akber (*i. e.* Akber the Great) was the best of all the emperors of Hindoostan, and to none was fitted the royal robe to a greater degree of propriety than to him, and that when his empire had reached to its highest glory, the English had taken possession of the ships sent by the emperor to Hejaz in Arabia, and notwithstanding the greatness of his power and might, and the English having had not the least power in India at that time, he could not take back the ships from the English nation. Now the English nation having brought the whole of India from the shores of the ocean to Peshawur under their rule, who is there that can dare set himself in opposition to these brave and wise rulers of this time.

The delay which has taken place in inflicting on the rebels the just retribution they deserve is not to be traced to the causes given out by the ignorant vulgar; but that this delay has been made on purpose in order to make a distinction between friends and enemies, between the wise and the foolish, and for other objects which the Government have in view.

Up to the time when the rebel troops entered Delhi nothing had happened from the part of the servants of the King displeasing to the English Government; but it is difficult to say what has caused a sudden change in these royal officers after the entrance of the rebel troops in Delhi, or what is the reasonable ground upon which they have set their hopes in siding with the rebels.

If the vain thoughts of the rebel sepoys have not touched you as yet, then it is equally difficult to understand what has prevented you from communicating your opinions to this camp and in endeavouring to put down this tumultuous disturbance. If there are some faithful servants of the King, then what is the reason that they negligently suffer the lamp of Hindostan (*i. e.* the King of Delhi), to be extinguished? And do not use all their best endeavours to keep its light as before? The way of doing this, in my opinion, is as follows:—The Ahulkars of the King ought, if they agree to my opinion, to communicate all their wishes and plans and those of his Majesty to the English officer in this camp, either personally or through a vakeel, in writing or verbally. It is worthy of being thought upon that when the rebels are punished and exterminated, and all things are settled, then it will not be the proper time for you to write and speak to the English officers. I wait for your answer, which, whatever it may be, will be laid before the English officer in this camp.

"I have broken the pen and shortened the subject.
For it is not in my way to speak in great length."

19*th October*, 1857.—Narrative of Khajah Khan Raus, Mouzah Warajaub Hussun, Affghan, Thanadar of Peshawur, who accompanied General Nicholson: also favourite personal orderly who stormed with him the breach at Delhi.

At four o'clock in the morning of the 14th September, 1857, General Nicholson got ready the entire column and advanced towards the Cashmere Gate. Having reached the place where the Government batteries were thrown up, the General moved to the assault, keeping on the right side of the column. To the east was the Cashmere Gate, where a breach had been made in the city wall by the cannon balls; he mounted the wall, charged, and took several of the enemy's batteries. Advancing in the direction of Skinner's house he there captured several other batteries. After that one of the villains shot him at a battery with a musket. The ball entered the right side under the arm-pit and came out under the left arm-pit. The General then desired to be laid in the shade, and said 'I will remain here till Delhi is taken.' He then called for some cold water. At that time I ordered a doolie from Delhi and sent Lateef Khan (with the General) to the General Hospital in camp, where Dr. ——— gave him some medicine, and he became a little better. He then ordered me to remove him to Major Daly's tent. Accordingly I removed him to the tent. On the next day the Sahib told me to give his salaam to Captain Lake, on the Mooltan Rassala, and ask whether the rebels still remained in Teliwarah and Kishungunge, or had been defeated. I went to Captain Lake and gave the salaam. The Captain mounted his horse and rode to see the General. General Nicholson wrote about Telliwarah and Kishungunge some thing with his own hand on a piece of paper, and gave it to the captain. To this letter the captain gave a verbal reply in English. The reason of the General's writing was that he had a severe pain in the abdomen, and had no strength left. After that, Captain Lake mounted and rode to his Rassala and gave some orders about the two places mentioned. On the 3rd day General Nicholson sent for Brigadier General Chamberlain, and talked with him also in English about Kishungunge and Salimghur. After that day Chamberlain himself went to the city and gave orders about Salimghur, and ordered the guns to open fire. On the 4th day, by orders of the doctor, the General was removed to an empty house in camp. On the 20th September the victory at Delhi was complete, the faces of the rebels were blackened, and they fled. I went to the Sahib and told him of the victory. He was greatly delighted, and said, 'My desire was that Delhi might be taken before I die, and it has been so.' On the 24th September, the (nightingale-faced) Sahib took his flight from this transitory world. After his death General Chamberlain and some English gentlemen came and cut each a lock of hair from his head. The body of the Sahib remained the day in the bungalow. In the morning at sunrise several of the Horse Artillery came and took the General's coffin and placed it on a bier behind the horses, and carried it once more towards the Cashmere Gate. They made him a grave in front of the Cashmere Gate between the two roads by which the assault was made. Brigadier Chamberlain, Brigade Major ———, ——— ———, and some other distinguished officers, and also Mr. Saunders, the Commissioner, came and did reverence to the body, and having taken up the coffin placed it in the grave. Utta Mahomed Khan, and Nowrung Khan, Russaldar of the Mooltan Horse, who was also present, asked Brigadier Chamberlain how the grave was to be made. The brigadier ordered it to be built with bricks within and raised high. Accordingly at that time the bricklayers set to work to prepare the place. When I went next morning to see the grave the building was raised as high as the coffin, and was finished with lime. And after the victory all the Sahibs went to the palace (the red fort) and remained there night and day.

Thus closed a career of the brightest promise. It culminated like a star; all eyes were turned to it admiringly, and it suddenly closed, not in darkness or in gloom—but in glory!

Troops of friends bore him to his grave. He had died the most envied of all deaths—the soldier's—in the hour and within hearing of the shouts of victory!

The following Appendices testify to the successful exertions of the Punjab Government to supply the places left by the exodus from its territories.

APPENDIX B.

MEMORANDUM of NATIVE TROOPS entertained in the PUNJAB, and additions to the Old Regiments, as per latest Returns received.

Regiments.	Date of Return.	Recruits enlisted. Mahomedans.	Sikhs.	Hill Men.	Total.
Horse, Guide Corps, Foot } Delhi	—	—	—	—	— *a*
4th Sikh Regt., Delhi	1 Sept.	—	—	—	124
1st Punjab Regt.	—	—	—	—	—
2nd ,,	—	—	—	—	233
4th ,, ,, Markunda	1 Sept.	—	—	—	— *b*
7th ,, ,, Meerut	15 Sept.	—	—	—	797
8th ,, ,, Noushera	,,	—	—	—	748
9th ,, ,, Kohat	1 Sept.	—	—	—	646
10th ,, ,, ,,	—	—	—	—	701
11th ,, ,, ,,	—	—	—	—	606
12th ,, ,, Lahore	1 Sept.	—	—	—	645
13th ,, ,, Seeplee	,,	—	—	—	727
16th ,, ,, ,,	—	—	—	—	646
17th ,, ,, Meean Meer	15 Sept.	—	—	—	797
18th ,, ,, Peshawur	,,	—	—	—	898
19th ,, ,, Rawul Pindee	,,	—	—	—	818
20th ,, ,, Ferozepore	,,	—	—	—	695
21st ,, ,, ,,	—	—	—	—	794
22nd ,, ,, Loodianah	15 Sept.	—	—	—	853
23rd ,, ,, ,,	—	—	—	—	777
1st Regt. S. I. Cav., Lahore	1 Oct.	—	—	—	583
14th Regt. Punjab Inf., Peshawur	—	—	—	—	— *a*
Recruiting Depot, 4th S. I.	—	—	—	—	143*c*
Landour Levy, Landour	—	—	—	—	82
Total	—	—	—	—	12,313

(*a*) No return. (*b*) No extra establishment. (*c*) At Phillour.

APPENDIX C.

MEMORANDUM of IRREGULAR HORSE and POLICEMEN entertained by the Judicial Commissioner for the N. W. P., and sent to their destination up to the 12th inst.

	Officers.	Men.	Total.
For Lieutenant Hodson's Irregular Horse	50	376	426
,, Sirsa District	35	506	341
,, Hissar District	16	250	266
,, Delhi District	14	226	240
Total	115	1,358	1,473

APPENDIX D.

MEMORANDUM of HORSE LEVIES entertained in the several Districts in the Punjab, as per latest Returns received.

Lahore, 10*th Oct.*, 1857.

Districts.	Date of Return.	Recruits entertained.			
		Mahomedans.	Sikhs.	Hill Men.	Total.
Peshawur	5 Sept.	1,012	306	—	1,318
Kohat	1 Oct.	209	3	11	223
Huzarah	1 Aug.	149	1	—	150
Leia	23 Sept.	30	3	—	33
Dera Ismael Khan	15 Sept.	36	93	535	664
Dera Ghazee Khan	3 Oct.	306	—	—	306
Mooltan	,,	—	—	—	112*a*
Jhung	1 Oct.	95	7	1	103
Goojaira	15 Aug.	—	—	—	57
Jhelum	30 Sept.	61	2	—	63
Rawul Pindee	5 Oct.	81	1	3	85
Shahpoor	1 Oct.	104	1	4	109
Goojerat	,,	83	4	9	96
Lahore	—	—	—	—	672*b*
Goojranwallah	1 Oct.	9	10	9	28*b*
Jullunder	30 Sept.	35	45	16	96*c*
Hooshearpoor	1 Oct.	8	80	10	98*d*
Kangra	15 Sept.	3	—	8	11
Rajah Jowahir Singh's Contingent	1 Oct.	—	—	—	14*e*
Sher Malick Mahomed Khan, Tawanah	—	295	—	3	298*f*
Surfraz Khan and Abdoolla Khan's Esa Khiel	—	—	—	—	114*e*
Futteh Shu Khan, Tawanah	—	—	—	—	332*e*
Khairooddeen Khan Kussooreah	—	—	—	—	112*e*
Sahib Khan, Tawanah	—	—	—	—	250*g*
Mooltanee Horse, under Lieut. Lind.	15 Aug.	—	—	—	355*h*
Mustapha Khan Khagwanee	1 Oct.	—	—	—	116*e*
Surfraz Khan Lukozye	—	—	—	—	100*e*
Haffizoolah Khan Wazar Khanee	1 Oct.	—	—	—	63*e*
Riza Mahomed Khan of Tak	—	—	—	—	68*i*
Mahomed Surfraz Khan	1 Sept.	—	—	—	54*i*
Sirdar Mahomed Ufzul Khan	—	—	—	—	157*i*
Sooltan Jan's Ressalah, under Lieut. Smith	—	—	—	—	112*k*
Alum Shu Khan's Tawanah Ressalah,	—	—	—	—	103*l*
attached to 21st P.I. Regt.	1 Oct.	—	—	—	68*m*
Meer Moobarick Shah's Ressalah, attached to 1st P. Inf.	—	—	—	—	80*h*
Osman Khan's Ressalah, Ferozepore	1 Oct.	—	—	—	60*e*
Total	—	—	—	—	6,660

(*a*) Extra Ressalah of Mounted Police.
(*b*) Mounted Police raised by Capt. Lawrence, 1 ress. sent to join the Guide Corps; 2½ on duty between Umballa and Delhi; 1 with the Jummoo Contingent.
(*c*) Mounted Police. (*d*) Levies. (*e*) With Gen. Van Cortlandt's Force.
(*f*) Jullunder. (*g*) Moveable Column. (*h*) At Delhi.
(*i*) Under Maj. Stokes at Meerut. (*k*) On duty at Meerut. (*l*) Ditto at Umballa.
(*m*) Under Capt. Obbard.

APPENDIX E.

MEMORANDUM of FOOT LEVIES entertained in the several Districts in the Punjab, as per latest returns received.

Lahore, Oct., 1857.

Districts.	Date of Return.	No. of all Ranks.	Remarks.
Peshawur	5 Sept.	1,438	
Kohab	1 Oct.	279	
Hazarah	1 Aug.	500	
Ditto, Sultee Comp.		46	
Leia	23 Sept.	253	
Dera Ismael Khan . .	18 Sept.	1,193	
Dera Ghazee Khan .	3 Oct.	338	
Mooltan	30 Sept.	24	
Goojaira	1 Sept.	449	
Jhelum	1 Oct.	147	Sanctioned strength, 400 ; reduced by transfer to New Punjab Regts.
Sealkote	,,	456	
Goojranwallah . .	,,	282	N. W. P.
Goordaspoor	,,	306	65 recruits for N. W. P.
Jullunder	,,	190	109 ditto.
Besides the following for Field Service :—			
Rajah Jowahir Singh's Contingent	,,	627	With Gen. Van Cortlandt's Force.
Mooltanee Irregulars .	,,	250	With Lt. Lind, with Delhi Field Force.
Haffizoolah Hazir Khanee	,,	170	With Van Cortlandt's Field Force.
Muzlee Pioneers . .	,,	1,013	With Lieut. Gulliver at Delhi.
Sikh Artillery, sent to Delhi and Loodianah	—	about 400	Employed at Delhi, and with Van Cortlandt's Field Force.
Loodianah	—	—	8 recruits for N. W. P.
Hoshiarpoor . . .	—	—	72 ditto.
Total . .	—	8,341	

London: Printed by SMITH, ELDER, and Co., Little Green Arbour Court, E.C.